·SHE·
THE BOOK OF THE GODDESS

Topaz Linda Garland 94

·SHE·
THE BOOK OF THE GODDESS

TEXT BY NIGEL SUCKLING

ILLUSTRATED BY LINDA & ROGER GARLAND

Linda Garland.   *Roger Garland '98*

Lakeside Gallery
Lezant , Launceston
Cornwall PL15 9NW UK
Web site : http://www.lakeside-gallery.com

First Published by Lakeside Gallery 1998

ISBN   0 9533841 0 1

Art Directors : Linda Garland, Roger Garland, Seth Garland

Printed by : Midas Printing Limited, Hong Kong

◁Previous page
Topaz
Linda 1994
Oils. 8 x 11in (20 x 28cm)

▷ Overleaf
Cybele and Calypso
Roger 1997
Oils. 20 x 14in (51 x 36cm)

CONTENTS

INTRODUCTION

To many people mythology seems a pointless study, a crock of mistaken beliefs on a par with, say alchemy in its relevance to modern life. To some, the tales are simply quaint and exotic fantasies, beautiful or terrifying fairytales about people and places that have only ever existed in dreams. And this is partly why we have gathered these tales, for the beauty and wonder of them. But we also believe these myths of goddesses from around the world still have much to say. Particularly in this age of global realignment between the genders. In the past such shifts of power and relationship were reflected in myths about conflict between the gods and goddesses. On some plane of the imagination similar dramas are probably being acted out now, though what shape they will take is tomorrow's surprise.

Myths are the distilled wisdom of the cultures that give them birth, attempts to come to grips with the unknown and give it a form that can be addressed. The language they use is the language of poetry, dream and vision. It is not always not easy to comprehend on an everyday level, but luckily that is often not needed. Sometimes one does not even want to try. Waking in the morning from a beautiful dream, it is not necessary to know what the dream 'means' for its mood to persist into the day. Often all that is required is to bear it in mind, mull over the details, and the mood follows even when insight does not.

Myths are cultural dreams and because of that can address a wide audience. Individual dreams employ many symbols that have meaning only to the dreamer, but myths use symbols that signify more or less the same to all who share in them. The beauty of the old tales is that they evolved slowly from generation to generation. Their message is well-honed, and they address many human preoccupations that have hardly changed since the beginning - birth, marriage and death, joy and grief, sanity and madness.

Some things do change of course. Many myths were addressed to agricultural societies intricately bound to the cycle of the seasons, which most of us are not. Our diet changes only slightly with the seasons, we have central heating and air conditioning. We expect to live out at least our three score and ten almost as a right. Most of us have no idea offhand what phase the moon is in, although in the past that was as inexorable as the date. Myths also assume the existence of a spiritual, dreamlike dimension overlapping and bound up with our own, which is a concept that has become almost alien in our age. So some preoccupations and preconceptions have changed from the times in which these tales took shape, but our instincts and emotions are still attuned to primaeval rhythms. We suffer if we ignore them too long. And it is these instinctual rhythms that are particularly addressed by the goddesses in the world pantheon.

Goddesses have tended to be overshadowed in the great world religions. All the evidence suggests that most cultures were originally matriarchal, but you have to dig deep to grasp what that must have been like. The Great Mother was usually demonized after her overthrow, or at least patronized. Her surviving legends were recorded by male hands and often layers of disinformation have to be peeled away to get the true picture. But as, say, Esther Harding has shown in her books, and Robert Graves in the White Goddess, there is plenty of material there if you look at it the right way. Even Lilith, one of the most demonized goddesses of all, has survived well enough for us to hazard a guess at how her side of the story might sound in a divorce court.

Which is not to say that the matriarchal goddesses were all light. Like the moon, the Great Mother had a dark phase. Danann became Black Annis, Selene became Hecate. Many goddesses are known to us only by their shadows; but if we recognize that this is so, the veil of Isis begins to draw aside.

1
CREATION

Creation myths are the foundation of every culture or religion. They all claim absolute truth, each contradicting the other and giving sceptics grounds enough for dismissing them all. But that is missing the point. As cultural dreams, creation myths are bound to contradict each other on the surface, just as the dogmas of organized religion do. Inspiration is bound to be shaped and interpreted differently by different people. The way it is shaped tells us much about those people and how they differ in cultural outlook. But if we look deeper, diving below the tangle of contradictions on the surface, what we find is an underlying unity. The springs of inspiration are the same for all cultures. The interpretation is what divides people. Conflicts arise when the interpretation is mistaken for a literal truth, which has happened all too often.

All creation myths have the same aim: to tell people where they came from and how they relate to the rest of creation. They outline the origins and spiritual evolution of their culture. For those accustomed to the tradition of a male creator of the universe, it may be refreshing to hear a few creation myths in which a goddess was the prime mover.

LUONNOTAR

The Kalevala is the national epic of Finland. Its tales have been recited round winter fires for thousands of years in the frozen north, but were not gathered into a coherent whole until the nineteenth century. The saviour of the tradition was Elias Lönnrot (1802 - 1884) who spent many years collecting folktales in northeast Finland. Then in a piece of inspired scholarship and poetry he welded the many strands together and published his definitive version in 1849.

◁ **The Kalevala**
Linda 1997
Oils. 11 x 15in (28 x 28cm)

As Finland was then struggling to break free of the influence of the Russians on one side and the Swedes on the other, the Kalevala was immediately seized upon as a focus for national identity. Few could actually read it at first because very few Finns spoke their own language, but over the next few decades the Kalevala played an enormous part in stimulating the rebirth of Finnish as a living language. Large portions of it were learned by heart.

The story of Creation in the Kalevala begins with Goldeneye, a sacred bird said to be a teal, flying over the dim ocean looking for a place to rest. But at that time there was no land, neither was there any sun or moon. There existed only the dim sky and the endless ocean. Then Luonnotar, mother of the water, virgin of the air, took pity and raised her knee from the cold waters as a perch for Goldeneye. The teal circled around and, thinking it a turf-grown cliff, settled down on Luonnotar's knee. There she built a nest and laid seven eggs, six of gold and one of iron:

O'er her eggs the teal sat brooding,
And the knee grew warm beneath her;
And she sat one day, a second,
Brooded also on the third day;

Then the Mother of the Waters,
Water-Mother, maid of the air,
Felt it hot, and felt it hotter,
And she felt her skin was heated,

Till she thought her knee was burning,
And that all her veins were melting.
Then she jerked her knee suddenly,
And her limbs convulsive shaking,

Rolled the eggs into the water,
Down amid the waves of ocean,
And to splinters they were broken,
And to fragments they were shattered.

But in ooze they were not wasted,
Nor the fragments lost in water,
But a wondrous change came o'er them,
And the fragments were transformed.

From a cracked egg's lower fragment
Was created the earth beneath,
From the top half of another
Rose the lofty arch of heaven.

From a yolk, the upper portion,
Began to glow just like the sun,
From a white, the upper portion,
Rose the moon that shines so brightly;

Whatso in the egg was mottled,
Now became the stars in heaven,
Whatso in the egg was blackish,
In the sky as cloudlets floated. ...

When the ninth year had passed over,
And the summer tenth was passing,
From the sea her head she lifted,
And her forehead she uplifted,

And she then began Creation,
And she brought the world to order,
On the open ocean's surface,
On the far extending waters.

Wheresoe'er her hand she pointed,
There she formed the jutting headlands;
Wheresoe'er her feet she rested,
There she formed the caves for fishes;

When she dived beneath the water,
There she formed the depths of ocean;
When towards the land she turned her,
There the level shores extended,

Where her feet to land extended,
Spots were formed for salmon-netting;
Where her head the land touched lightly,
There the curving bays extended.

LILITH

Legend has it that Lilith was Adam's first wife, created together with him on the Sixth Day and from the same materials. Some say Lilith was created a little later, after Adam complained to God that he alone of the creatures of the earth had no partner. Either way, Lilith was created independently from and of the same materials as Adam. They were equals, and this led to problems.

Not least of their difficulties, it is said, arose because Adam always liked to be on top when making love. No doubt this was merely a symptom of deeper differences, but it was the issue that caused the rift in the end. After a particularly fierce argument which Adam attempted tried to win by force, Lilith in fury uttered the mystical, ineffable Name of the Almighty, clapped her hands and flew away.

Adam complained to Jehovah that he had been abandoned, so God sent three angels to persuade Lilith to return home. The angels found Lilith on the shores of the Red, Sea in an area populated by a particularly lascivious breed of demon, from whose attentions she had been giving birth to more little demons at the rate of a hundred a day. At least, that is how the angels reported

▷ **Lilith**
Linda 1998
Oils 13 x 18in (33 x 46cm)

it. One has to bear in mind that this is the tale told from Adam's point of view. Imagination is required for the other side of the story.

The three angels tried to coax Lilith to return to Adam but she only laughed scornfully saying: 'How could I go back to live with Adam after the entertainment I have enjoyed here?' The angels threatened to kill her but again Lilith only laughed and dared them to try. Which they did, and failed. But after a great struggle they managed to bundle her into the Outer Darkness and slaughter her offspring.

Adam meanwhile had been provided with a new mate in the form of Eve, who was fashioned from his rib in the hope that this would bind her more closely to him. And the rest of their tale is well enough known not to need repeating here.

In the Outer Darkness Lilith, whose most common form was of a woman from the waist up and a serpent below, became the consort of Samael and other fallen angels. Fury with Adam and grief for her slaughtered children led Lilith to plot revenge. By mating with the rebel angels in the Outer Darkness she is said to have brought into being many of the greatest demons to plague the world. Chief among them were the lilin or lamiae of the ancient world, vampires who are also known as succubi, fatal seducers of men and devourers of new-born children.

Lilith was banished from the world of Adam and Eve but she occasionally managed to sneak back. It is often said that the serpent which tempted Eve in the Garden of Eden was none other than Lilith. Many Medieval scenes of the Temptation show the serpent as female from the waist up and handing the fatal apple to Eve, thus helping bring about the Fall.

Her offspring also continued to plague Adam's descendants whenever possible. As succubi their favourite ploy was to seduce men in their sleep and steal their semen for the creation of more demons. Or sometimes they would reverse gender and become male incubi who ravished lonely women, impregnating them with the stolen seed and causing them to give birth to monsters. To guard against being seduced in their sleep like this, single men especially used to keep by the bed a bowl or cup engraved with an image of Lilith surrounded by the names of the angels who had originally banished her - Senoy, Sansenoy and Semangelof. This was believed to be enough to frighten the succubi away and prevent 'wet dreams'.

The destruction of her children by the angels left Lilith with a terrible passion for revenge against the children of Adam and Eve. She sought to destroy them at birth by strangling or suffocating them, or drinking their blood. Among Jews the greatest danger was reckoned to be, for boys, up to the eighth day after birth when they were circumcised; among baby girls the period of greatest danger lasted until the twentieth day. Among other measures used to ward off the evil were amulets bearing the names of the three angels who cast Lilith out.

The screech owl is Lilith's totem bird. It is the form in which she often prowls the night in search of freshborn humans. Most commonly she appears as a beautiful female from the waist up and a serpent below, but has been represented as a voluptuous human with wings and owl's feet. When seducing men she is of course able to disguise her true appearance by glamour.

The legend of Lilith is a dark and grim one, but it gives a glimpse into a long buried strata of the feminine in Jewish legend. This filtered into Christian mythology too, in the form of Gnostic legends which tell of God himself having a heavenly consort, and daughters such as Sophia, the Wisdom of God, to whom countless Eastern churches are dedicated.

THE BABYLONIAN CREATION MYTH

The ancient Babylonian or Akkadian creation epic has survived on seven tablets known as the Enuma Elish, this title coming from the opening words: 'When on high . . .' This version dates from at least 2,000 BC but tells a story that is far older, and which was recited in public on the fourth day of every Babylonian New Year festival to remind people of their origins. The Enuma Elish tells us that all creation sprang from the mixing of two primal elements, sweet and salt water, known as Apsu and Tiamat. These elements were also deities, the original divine couple and this is the tale of how, through them, all things came into being.

When on high the heaven had not been named, nor the earth below, there existed naught but Tiamat, the mother of all things, and Apsu, the begetter. Then through the mingling of their waters were the first gods created, Mummu the god of spray, and Lahmu and Lahamu who were serpents. Then came Kishar the earth goddess and Anshar the sky god, and many others including Ea who became their leader.

These goddesses and gods rejoiced in their fresh existence, but their laughter and songs and games in heaven soon annoyed Tiamat and Apsu, who were unused to such din. Finally Apsu went to resplendent Tiamat and complained: Their ways are loathsome to me. By day I find no relief, nor repose by night. We must destroy them to get some peace. Let us have rest and quiet again.'

Tiamat was appalled: 'What, should we destroy all our children? I agree they are boisterous and it is hard to find any peace since they came, but let's be patient and perhaps in time they'll calm down.'

Reluctantly Apsu agreed, but later his vizier Mummu persuaded him back to his first impulse. Secretly they plotted the death of all the noisy upstarts, but rumours reached the threatened ones. Ea the all-wise divined the scheme and against it devised a plan of his own. He forged a spell that cast Apsu into a deep sleep. Then Ea removed his crown, placed it on his own head and killed Apsu as he lay. And from Apsu's bones he built himself a tabernacle where he lived and ruled over the other gods in splendour with Damkina, his wife.

To Ea and Damkina was born a son, and the goddess' milk filled him with beauty and strength. Ea was proud of his son, he exulted and glowed and his heart filled with gladness. He named the child Marduk, though sometimes also he is also known as Bel or Baal. Deeming Marduk perfect, Ea set him above all the other gods to rule as he saw fit.

Four were Marduk's eyes, four his ears and when he opened his mouth fire poured forth. He was taller than mountains and shone like the sun. To Marduk was given power over the four winds and the hurricane, and he played with them as a child plays with its toys.

Then many of the other gods grew jealous of Marduk and angry at his high-handedness with them. They took their complaints to Tiamat. They begged her also to remember Apsu, her husband, and how cruelly he had been murdered by Ea while she had just stood by doing nothing. So Tiamat was finally moved to seek revenge. She formed a council of the rebels to prepare for war.

While the war council made plans, Mother Hubur, she who fashions all things (and who some say was but another form of Tiamat herself), gave birth to eleven kinds of monster to help the battle: 'serpents, sharp of tooth, unsparing of fang. With venom for blood she has filled their bodies. Roaring dragons she has clothed with terror, has crowned them with haloes, making them like gods, so that he who beholds them shall perish abjectly, and that, with their bodies reared up, none might turn them back. She has set up the Viper, the Dragon, and the Sphinx, the Great-Lion, the Mad-Dog, and the Scorpion-Man, mighty lion-demons, the Dragon-Fly, the Centaur; bearing weapons that spare not, fearless in battle.'

From among her assembly Tiamat elevated Kingu to be her new consort and battle-leader, and fastened to his breast the Tablet of Destinies. He was given the rank of Anu.

When Ea heard of these preparations for war, he went to his forefather Anshar for advice, and together they too gathered an army and prepared for battle. But first they decided to send a champion to face Tiamat and see if the dispute could be settled by single combat. All agreed it was a good plan but none had the courage to face Tiamat till at last Anshar thought of Marduk, the greatest of champions and cause of all the trouble in the first place. Marduk was summoned and when he had heard the situation he laughed lightly and said:

'What are you all afraid of? This is no great warrior we face. It is but Tiamat, a woman. You shall soon tread upon her neck.' He agreed to take on the challenge, but only if he was formally accepted as king of all gods on their side, even Ea himself. This was soon agreed, for if none but Marduk was brave enough to face Tiamat, how should he not be their king? A great feast was held to enthrone Marduk. Ea and all his followers swore loyalty, then Marduk armed himself with the four winds, the cyclone, the hurricane, lightning and many other weapons:

'He mounted the storm-chariot irresistible and terrifying. He harnessed and yoked to it a team-of-four, the Killer, the Relentless, the Trampler, the Swift. Their lips were parted, their teeth bore poison. They were tireless and skilled in destruction. On his right he posted the Smiter, fearsome in battle, on the left the Combat, which repels all the zealous. For a cloak he was wrapped in an armor of terror; with his fearsome halo his head was turbaned. The lord went forth and followed his course, towards the raging Tiamat he set his face.'

Marduk rode into Tiamat's camp and challenged her to single combat. Battle commenced and did not last long, for Marduk quickly released an evil wind that tore into Tiamat through her mouth. While she struggled to contain it, Marduk cast a net over her, drew out his bow and finished Tiamat with an enchanted arrow that split her heart in two. And with this blow the courage drained from Tiamat's followers. Marduk rounded them all up, including the terrifying beasts, and either killed them or bound them till he should decide their fate. Kingu he also subdued, taking from him the Tablet of Destinies and fastening it to his own breast.

Thus did Marduk achieve mastery of all creation. Turning back to the body of Tiamat, he considered what to do next. He split the body like a shellfish in two. Half of it he raised as the firmament of the sky, the other half became the earth. From her eyes flow the two great rivers Tigris and Euphrates. In the firmament he assigned places for the greater gods and marked them with stars. He established the zodiac and determined their courses. From the spittle of Tiamat he created clouds and filled them with rain. And he created also the animals that fill the earth, the birds that fly above, the fish that swim beneath. And from the blood of Kingu, who was sacrificed for this purpose, humans were created to honour and serve the gods.

Thus did Marduk create heaven and earth as we know them from the body of Tiamat, the Great Mother. Then he returned to his father and at the gate of Apsu he set Tiamat's eleven creatures as statues, as a reminder of all he had done. Then he ascended his throne and from that day was supreme ruler of the gods. And he renamed Apsu Babylon, which means 'the houses of the great gods'.

To the ancient Babylonians who recited this tale every new year, what it represented was the triumph of order over primeval chaos. Historians see it reflecting the overthrow of matriarchal religion and rule by the bright new god of male supremacy. But to give Marduk's followers their due, they did not demonize Tiamat to the usual extent; unlike, say, Lilith by the Israelites. Tiamat's body becomes the raw stuff of Marduk's creation, and she is still recognized as the prime mother of all beings, including Marduk himself.

△ **Tiamat**
Linda 1998
Watercolour (actual size)

◁ **Marduk**
Roger 1998
Pencil 10 x 8in (25 x 20cm)

The Egg and the Tree of Life

The female side is often played down in Creation myths, but by the very nature of things it then surfaces elsewhere. New life springs from the union of male and female, the sky and the earth, the seed and the egg. This is an inescapable rule of life,

its definition even. Without the egg, the seed is no more than an abstract possibility, an untried idea. The egg is the matrix by which this potential enters life and is clothed in matter so it can go out and test itself against reality. The egg is the crucible of life, the forge of Creation.

All mythologies recognize this. Behind them all hangs a vision of the time before time, when the

World Egg floated in the Abyss, waiting to be quickened so that the universe could come into being.

They also recognize that the magnetism drawing seed and egg together is generally love and desire in all their complicated varieties. We are drawn into being by love, nurtured by the earth and given meaning by inspiration. These are three bright aspects of the Goddess - Aphrodite, Demeter and Artemis, say; or Venus, the Earth and the Moon.

In Christian tradition the near absence of the female in the story of Creation was compensated for by the Virgin Mary, Mother of God, and many other saints who stepped into the shoes of displaced pagan goddesses and continued their work. There is also a bow to the Goddess in the timing of Easter, which is determined by the first full moon after the Spring Equinox. Behind the Christian celebration of Jesus's resurrection lies, thinly veiled, the primordial celebration of Gaia's reawakening after winter. Easter even gets its name in English, according to the Venerable Bede, from the Anglo-Saxon moon and fertility goddess Eostre, whose festival was celebrated at the Spring Equinox.

Venus, the Earth and the Moon are aspects of the Goddess linked by the Tree of Life whose roots burrow deep into the earth, and whose branches net the sky across which the moon and stars travel. The Chaldean Hymn of Eridu, one of the oldest poems in existence, says of the Tree of Life:

> *Its roots of white crystal burrow towards the Deep.*
> *Its seat was the central place of the earth;*
> *Its foliage was the couch of Zikum, the First Mother.*
> *Into the hearth of the holy house, which spreads shade like a forest,*
> *Hath no man entered.*
> *There is the dwelling of the Mighty Mother*
> *Who passes across the sky.*

This is the tree that stood in the Garden of Eden, along with the Tree of the Knowledge of Good and Evil whose fruit Eve was tempted to eat. Far from being the disaster this is generally made out to be, with the attendant burden of guilt passed on to Eve's daughters, it can be argued that eating the fruit was essential for the evolution of consciousness. As long as the first couple simply obeyed God's laws they were children, or cattle with no real insight or command over their own lives. The knowledge they gained by eating the fruit was uncomfortable, but as even God admits in Genesis it conferred on Adam and Eve a degree of divinity that made them equal to the angels. They rose in consciousness and embarked upon their own drama. If the serpent who tempted Eve was Lilith, the temptation was how she passed on the torch of feminine consciousness to Eve to compensate for the overwhelming masculinity of Jehovah and Adam.

The two trees in Eden have often merged in the popular mind, and it is even possible that originally there was just the one tree with two names over which confusion later crept in. In north-western Europe Eve's fruit was understood to be an apple, the apple tree having long been held the noblest of the seven noble trees (hence 'Avalon, the Isle of the Apple Trees'). Fruit from the sacred apple tree confers immortality, it is a tree of life as well as knowledge.

◁ **Summer** (detail)
Linda 1977
Oils 9 x 9in (23 x 23cm)

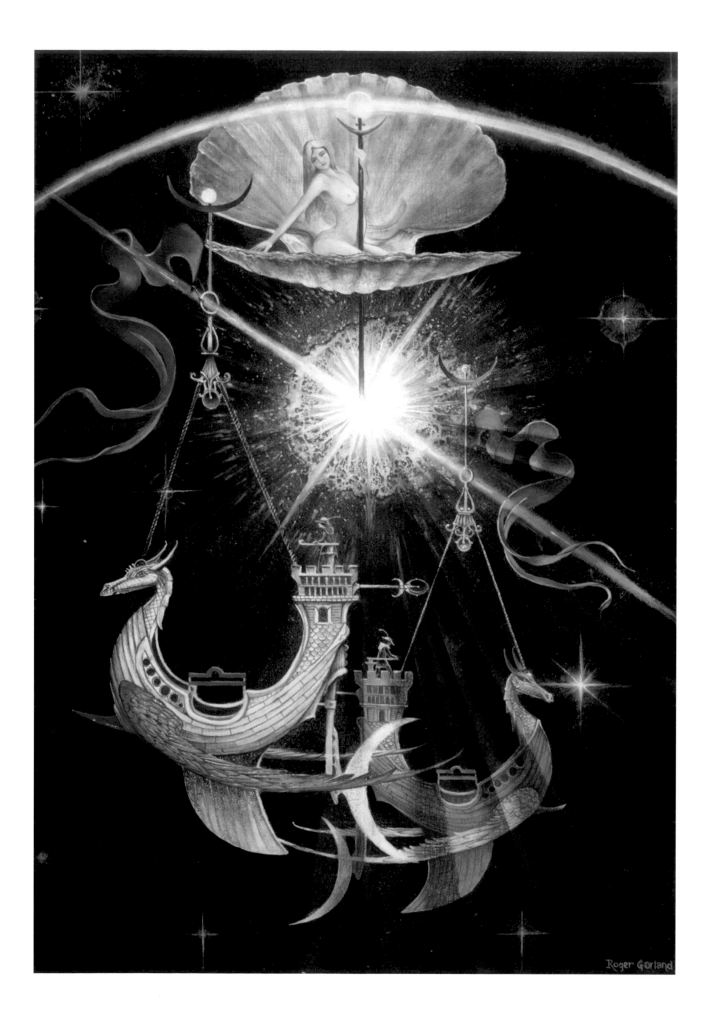

SUN 2 MOON & STARS

We forget how fascinating the sky was to our ancestors. The sun still figures largely in our lives and is even worshipped to a degree, especially by those of us in temperate climes among whom a visiting alien would still be forgiven for thinking sunbathing is some religious rite, despite recent ultraviolet scares.

The moon plays a more marginal part in most of our lives, and the stars a lesser role still. Even for most astrologers the actual stars in the night sky, as opposed to the notional ones in their charts, are little more than vague clusters of sparkling light. Occasionally on a balmy summer night we look up and are moved by the grandeur of the jewelled dome of heaven, but few of us can do more than point out the Pole Star, the Big Dipper and perhaps Orion's Belt.

To our ancestors the night sky was a living and omnipresent wonder. The patterns of the stars were as familiar as the faces of their loved ones. The wandering stars, or planets, caused the most speculation but the fixed constellations also generated myths to explain their origins, and it is curious how similar some of these myths are in totally different parts of the world.

An example is the tale of the Pleiades, a group of six or occasionally seven stars near Orion. Among both ancient Greeks and Native Americans these were said to be seven sisters. In Greek myth the seventh hides herself because she is Electra who cannot bear to look on the ruin of Troy, founded by her son Dardanus. Among Native Americans the seven sisters were said to descend to earth occasionally in a wicker basket to dance and sing by a lake. A young Indian fell in love with the youngest of them and won her as a bride from her father the Sun. Sometimes they live on earth and sometimes in the sky, which is why the star comes and goes.

As in this tale the sun is most commonly perceived as male and the moon female but it is not always so, as in Japan.

◁ **Tourmaline**
Roger 1997
Oils 10 x 8in (25 x 20cm)

Amaterasu, Goddess of the Sun

According to Japanese tradition preserved in the 8th century book Kojiki, when heaven and earth came into being, five kami or deities were born, chief of whom was Ame no Minakanushi (Master of the August Centre of Heaven). Below these five came seven generations of divine brother-sister couples. The seventh pair, Izanagi and Izanami, were charged by Ame no Minakanushi to consolidate the earth, which was then dim and formless and floated like jelly on the surface of the deep. So, standing on the Floating Bridge of Heaven, they dipped a spear through the clouds into the ocean and stirred until the island of Onogoro was formed. On this island they made love, and from their lovemaking sprang other islands and lesser gods of wind, mountains, trees and wind, and so on until the world was shaped. The last child they created together was the god of fire, and his birth was so painful that soon after Izanami died.

Izanagi was so distraught by Izanami's death that he went down to the underworld, Yomi no Kuni, to try and reclaim her. But he was met by her shade, who warned him it was too late because she had already tasted the food of the underworld so could not return. Izanagi pleaded and argued until she said she would go and try to reason with the god of hell. She begged Izanagi not to follow her but he was impatient and did so. Finally he came upon Izanami's decomposing body watched over by eight gods of thunder. Izanagi turned and fled in horror, pursued by all the gods and demons of hell. Finally he escaped and blocked the entrance to the underworld with a boulder.

As he staggered away, fresh gods sprang into being around Azanagi at almost every step. He threw away his stick and it became the god of crossroads. He threw away his clothes and they too became gods. He washed in the Tachibana river and the filth on him became gods of pestilence. He dived into the sea and from his bathing sprang all the gods of the ocean. Finally he bathed his left eye and gave birth to the goddess of the sun, Amaterasu O'kami, the Great August Shining Deity of Heaven, whom he placed in command of heaven. He bathed his right eye and gave birth to the god of the moon, Tsukiyomi, whom he gave command over the night. He bathed his nose and gave birth to the god Susanoo no Mikoto (the Troublesome, Swift Impetuous God), whom he gave command over the seas.

Amaterasu and Tsukiyomi accepted their duties happily, but Susanoo rebelled and said that instead he wanted to visit his 'mother' Izanami in the land of the dead. But first he wanted to visit his sister Amaterasu. So up to heaven he went, shaking the earth and mountains so alarmingly that his sister armed herself with a bow and arrows. When he arrived, Susanoo protested to her that he meant no harm and suggested that as proof of this they should make children together. So Amaterasu took his sword and broke it in three pieces, from which she created three goddesses. Then Susanoo took her five strings of jewels and from them created five gods. These eight offspring became the ancestors of the eight chief ruling families of Japan, and through them later emperors were to claim direct descent from Amaterasu herself.

This display of good intent obviously strained Susanoo too far however because afterwards he went on the rampage through heaven, destroying the rice fields and irrigation canals and temples dedicated to the first fruits. Like

△ **Japanese Landscape**
Roger 1998
Watercolour (actual size)

◁ **Amaterasu**
Linda 1998
Coloured pencils 20 x 14in (50 x 36cm)

many a partner, Amaterasu made excuses for this behaviour but finally he went too far. One day as she was weaving garments with her followers in the gods' house, Susanoo made a hole in the roof and dropped through it the flayed carcass of a horse. One of the weavers was so shocked she pricked herself with the point of her spindle and fell dead. Amaterasu fled and hid herself in a cave, blocking the door with a boulder that no-one else could move. Heaven and the world were plunged into darkness and hordes of evil demons rose from hell to plague them.

The good gods gathered in a dry riverbed to decide what to do, and between them a plan was formed. First they gathered all the cockerels they could find (because of course their crowing always attracts Amaterasu). Then a mirror was hung in a tree facing Amaterasu's hiding place, with jewels and ribbons decorating the branches. Then a tub was brought and placed upside down by the cavemouth and the goddess Ama no Uzume, clothed in vines and flowers and greenery, climbed onto the tub and began to dance. The drumming of her heels on the tub and the crowing of the cocks caught Amaterasu's attention. Then she heard applause and laughter, for the dancer, carried away in the ecstasy of her dance, began stripping off her clothes.

Amaterasu called out to know what was going on. Ama no Uzume replied that the gods were celebrating because a new goddess had come to take her place. Piqued, Amaterasu rolled back the stone a little to peep out. Seeing her own reflection in the mirror amidst the gaiety of jewels and ribbons, she took it for the glow of her rival. Rolling back the stone further, she leaned out for a closer look at the upstart and was seized and dragged out into the open, the cave being blocked against her return.

Thus light and warmth were restored to the world and the demons driven back into the shadows. As punishment for what he had done Susanoo had his beard, moustache and nails torn out and was banished from heaven. However he redeemed himself later by various heroic deeds on earth and eventually became a hero in his own right.

Every year the turning of the seasons recreates the drama of Amaterasu going into hiding and being to hide it from the sun. Hera detained the goddess of childbirth, so Leto was in labour for nine days and nights before giving birth to Artemis and Apollo. To avoid the same agony, Artemis vowed to remain a virgin forever; but equally she became a patron of women in childbirth and was called the Opener of the Womb'. Because of the birth of these shining twins the island was henceforth named Delose, the Brilliant'.

As Apollo's twin, Artemis was a moon-goddess and is often depicted with the crescent moon and stars around her head. But she ceded many of her moon-powers to Selene and is better known as a huntress. The first favour she asked of her father Zeus was for a silver bow and arrows. With these she loved nothing better than the joy of the chase, accompanied by her nymphs and hounds and female followers. Her symbol is a bear and she was known as Attis to the Celts. In appearance she is slim and virginal, with her hair usually tied back and wearing a light chiton ending at her knees, though sometimes it is longer. She was a fierce defender of her chastity, and many a youth who either fell in love with her or happened to see her naked came to a painful end. The hunter Actaeon was one who happened to come across her bathing after the hunt. Artemis changed him into a stag so he was torn to pieces by his own hounds.

Chastity was also strictly imposed on her followers. Any who strayed or even were tricked into losing their virginity met with her full fury. So

coaxed out again. Rice is a traditional offering to Amaterasu and mirrors are sacred to her.

Artemis, Selene and Hecate

Artemis (the Roman Diana) was the twin sister of Apollo and daughter of Leto and Zeus. When Leto became pregnant by Zeus she had to hide from the jealous fury of Zeus' wife Hera. From land after land Leto was turned away till finally she was accepted on the isle of Ortygia. Until then it had been a floating island but Poseidon now anchored it to the seabed. To fulfil Hera's curse that Leto could only give birth in a place where the sun's rays never shone, Poseidon raised a curtain of waves around and over

Artemis could be as fierce and vindictive at times as she was generous to those who pleased her, or sought her aid in some cause that she approved. She was also, like Apollo, a great musician and would sometimes put aside her bow, dress gaily and join him for joyous celebrations and dancing.

Artemis is often confused with an Asian goddess of the same name whose temple at Ephesus was one of the wonders of the ancient world. The confusion was perpetuated by the Romans who insisted on calling it the Temple of Diana at Ephesus. There was in fact no connection because the Artemis of Ephesus is usually portrayed as a sumptuously clothed and crowned fertility goddess with many breasts. When the temple was destroyed by fire its glow was visible for fifty miles.

More truly, however, Artemis was equated by the Greeks with Bast, the Egyptian cat-goddess.

SELENE

Selene was the daughter of the Titans Hyperion and Theia, and the sister of Helios, the sun god who preceded Apollo. Although not ranked among the twelve great gods and goddesses of Olympus, she was among those who considered themselves equal to them. And in fact, unlike her brother Helios, Selene was never really displaced by Artemis as goddess of the moon. Artemis merely took over one aspect of her, the crescent, virginal, new moon.

Selene was herself originally a triple goddess, but with Artemis on one side and Hecate on the other she came to be seen as the embodiment of the full moon.

As the full moon, Selene rises from her bed just as Helios descends from the sky. After bathing herself in the ocean she mounts the sky in a chariot drawn by shining steeds. It is said that one night as she was thus crossing the sky, she looked down and saw a prince, Endymion, asleep in a grotto after a day's hunting. Stooping to look closer, she fell in love with him and stole a kiss which bound them forever. To be her equal he asked Zeus for the gift of eternal youth and immortality, which Zeus granted. But as a condition he caused Endymion to fall into permanent sleep. So every night Selene guards him lovingly as he sleeps in his cave and he can join her only in his dreams. Some say he fathered fifty daughters on Selene before Zeus bestowed his mixed blessing of immortality.

Like Demeter, Selene is a goddess of fertility both on land and sea. She controls the rains, the tides of the ocean and also the tides of sap in growing things. More than this though, she is the goddess of wisdom and inspiration through the dreams she sends to mortals. And to those who displease her she is the sender of madness, or lunacy. Though this is normally the province of Hecate, whom the ancients feared.

HECATE

Hecate was goddess of both the moon and the underworld. She embodies the waning and dark moon. Hesiod described her as the daughter of the Titans Perses and Asteria, but later tradition said her parents were Zeus and Hera.

Hecate was one of the deities of Olympus until she angered Hera by giving her rouge to the nymph Europa, one of Zeus' extramarital lovers. Fleeing from Hera, Hecate drowned in the Acheron river and thus became one of the three principal deities of the underworld, along with Hades and Persephone. She was known as the Invincible Queen of the Dead and presided over purifications and penances.

Hecate could be generous; she bestowed prosperity, victory and wisdom on humans whom she favoured, was a guide to sailors and could send or withhold storms at will. But she was also quick to blight the life of anyone who offended her and, unlike Selene and Artemis, was more feared than loved. She was the goddess of magic and enchantment, and the queen of witches. She haunted crossroads and graveyards, where offerings to her were made and statues often set up to deflect her anger.

The time of a waning moon was considered unlucky for planting crops, or indeed beginning any enterprise that required fertility. The time of the dark moon was when Hecate's dark side was most to be feared, a time of sorcery and storms. In mid-August a great festival was held in Greece in which prayers and sacrifices were made so that Hecate would withhold storms that might ruin the harvest. This festival was Christianized as the Feast of the Assumption of the Virgin Mary and prayers for a good harvest are still offered at that time.

DANANN

The Irish Book of Invasions tells us that when the Gael arrived in Ireland they found it ruled by an elvish race known as the Tuatha de Danann, or 'Children of the Goddess Danann'. The Tuatha were said to have originally arrived riding through the sky in magical flying ships. They were described as: 'the most handsome and delightful company, the fairest of form, the most distinguished in their equipment and apparel, and their skill in music and playing, the most gifted in mind and temperament that ever came to Ireland. The Tuatha De excelled all the peoples of the world in their proficiency in every art.'

With the arrival of the Celtic Sons of Mil, the Tuatha withdrew into the Otherworld by way of the many sacred hills and fairy-mounds of Ireland, which remained gateways between the two realms. The interaction between the two peoples is the theme of countless ancient and modern Irish tales. Even into the twentieth century respectable witnesses would tell without fear of ridicule of their encounters with 'the gentry', particularly in the west of Ireland.

The Tuatha became the gods of the pagan Celts. Even after the arrival of Christianity the scribes who wrote down the old legends made no effort to deny their existence, although their divinity was of course played down. The scribes even admitted that the Tuatha most probably came from heaven, though whether as angels or fallen angels was disputed.

The goddess Danann, mother of the Tuatha, was also known as Dana, Danu, Anu, Anna and Annis. The name means Shining One, Goddess of the Moon. Her male counterpart, to begin with anyway, was the Dagda, or 'All Father', known also as 'The Good God'. Later he amiably handed his crown to his son, the solar Lugh. Whether the Dagda was son, husband or father to Danann is

not perfectly clear as different accounts suggest all three. There is also a blurring of distinction between Danann and Brigid, under which name the moon goddess was worshipped later; and Brigid is described as the Dagda's daughter as often as Danann is said to be his wife. Possibly, being a Triple Goddess, Danann was all three, Mother, Wife and Daughter in separate incarnations; but it may be that she was simply the Dagda's consort, and like him she was gradually replaced by one of her daughters.

COSMOGONY LEGEND OF THE SUN AND MOON

The Seres people of West Africa have this tale to account for the difference in brightness of the sun and the moon:

One day the Sun's mother and the Moon's mother were bathing themselves in a pool below a waterfall. Their children were playing nearby. The Sun was embarrassed by his mother's nakedness and turned his back so as not to see it. But the Moon was fascinated and crept closer through the bushes so that she might see all the better.

Later the Sun's mother called him and praised him for his tact and the respect it showed: 'And because you turned your eyes away and did not spy on me at the waterfall, I will ask the Great Spirit to arrange that no mortal creature should be able to look steadily at you.'

But the Moon's mother was angry and to her daughter she said: 'Because you did not show respect to me at the waterfall and stared long and hard at my nakedness, I will see to it that everyone can stare at you for as long as they like without tiring their eyes.'

Africa is home to many different people and many different accounts of how the sun, moon and stars came into being. The Bomitaba of Zaire say that the Moon and Sun were equally bright until one day the Sun suggested they take a swim. He pretended to dive in but caught himself on a branch above the pool. The Moon went sailing past into the water and her heat and half her light were extinguished. In Uganda they say that once upon a time the sky grew so crowded with the children of the Sun and Moon that they agreed to kill them all. But the Moon reneged on the deal which is why only her children, the stars, are now seen.

From South Africa comes this tale of the creation. In the beginning there existed for unmeasurable time nothing, till out of this nothingness emerged the Great Spirit, Unkulunkulu, and the great mother goddess Ma, who had the form of a gigantic woman. At Unkulunkulu's command Ma produced out of herself the earth, the sun and the stars. Then Ma sat down on a mountain to contemplate her creation; but she felt strangely unhappy. A great loneliness filled her that she had no-one to share it all with, and she began to weep great floods of tears from which came all the rivers and lakes of the world.

Seeing her unhappiness, Unkulunkulu, who is pure light, decided to provide Ma with a mate, and told her so. One morning she heard a strange voice calling out to her and full of excitement went racing through the mountains towards the sound of the voice, raising such clouds of dust that soon she could not see anything at all. Then she felt a touch and at first her heart leaped for joy, then recoiled in horror for it was not the gentle touch of any being like herself, but a grasping, probing, suffocating embrace of what seemed a thousand rough-skinned tentacles. Then through the settling dust she saw dozens of lust-filled eyes gazing upon her from a monstrous body where the tentacles merged. And from a wide mouth studded with jewels and minerals and lined with sharp fangs came the voice again: 'Submit to me, my love. I am the Tree of Life, I am your mate and I am aflame with desire!' With a shriek Ma broke free and fled across the face of the earth, pleading with Unkulunkulu to save her from the monster that chased her like an octopus racing across the seabed. Ma fled across the Kalahari Desert and dived into Lake Makarikari, but still the Tree of Life pressed hard behind her. Finally she climbed from the lake and flung herself into the sky, leaving the Tree of Life stranded on the shore. But he scooped up a mass of rock and clay from the lake bed, fashioned it into a vast ball and threw it after Ma. It struck her head and she fell helplessly back into his embrace. From their couplings she gave birth to all living creatures that walk, crawl, swim or fly above the earth.

The great ball of clay meanwhile rebounded into the sky where it has remained ever since as the moon. Lake Makarikari has since dried up and become a salt plain in Botswana.

△ **Dreamtime**
Linda 1988
Oils 7 x 7in (18 x 18cm)

ABORIGINAL MYTHS OF THE SUN AND MOON

Amongst the Aboriginal people of Australia the sun, Yhi, is female and the moon, Baiame, is male. The Narrinyeri of south Australia say that Yhi is compelled to visit the land of the dead every night and no amount of pleading by humans can change this. In return for a favour to humans she was presented with a red kangaroo skin which she wears when she comes and goes from the underworld, which accounts for her colour at dawn and sunset.

For a long time, say most Aboriginals, there was no sun, only the moon and stars. The birds and beasts were larger in that age and different to how they are now. The kangaroo had no tail and walked on all fours, the crocodile and the lizard had no patterns on their backs, the anteater had no spines and the turtle no shell.

These things came only later, and there are tales explaining how it happened. (The kangaroo acquired its tail when a bandicoot latched onto its bottom and would just not let go; and it learnt to hop the way it does when escaping from a fire with burned front paws.)

How the sun came into being was something like this: One day on the plain by the Murrimbidgee River, Dinewan the emu and Brolga, one of the first women, started arguing over a grinding stone the emu had stolen. And from arguing they progressed to quarrelling, and from quarrelling they fell to fighting. Finally in a rage Brolga ran to Dinewan's nest, seized one of the huge eggs there and hurled it into the sky. Up there it shattered over a heap of kindlewood that burst into flame, creating daylight for the first time. All creatures below were astonished, because in the dim light before they had not appreciated half the beauty of their world. The goddess Yhi was astonished too and took it upon herself to keep the flame alight. According to some accounts this is why she returns to the underworld each night, to build a new bonfire for the next day with the help of her attendant spirits. When the pile of wood is ready she sends out the Morning Star to warn that it is about to be lit with the last spark of the previous day's fire.

Not enough people on earth noticed this sign however, because they were of course asleep and had their eyes tight shut. So Yhi pondered a long while what other sign there could be to warn of her coming. Then one evening she heard the laughter of Googoorgaga, the laughing jackass, echoing over the plain. 'That is the sign we want,' she said.

She went to Googoorgaga and told him to keep watch for the Morning Star, instructing him that when the star began to fade he was to laugh his loudest and wake all the sleepers for sunrise. To make sure he did this, Yhi warned the Googoorgaga that if he ever failed in his duty she would not light the fire then or ever again, and he would suffer along with the rest.

Aborigine children are forbidden to imitate the Googoorgaga's call in case they confuse him so he neglects his duty and darkness returns forever. Those children who do, grow an extra tooth above their eye tooth as punishment for what they have done.

3

ELEMENT EARTH

Earth is the aspect of the Goddess that mattered most to our agrarian ancestors whose first priority was getting enough to eat. They studied the moods of the Earth Goddess minutely and had countless ways of propitiating her and coaxing forth her abundance. In pagan times the Earth Goddess was openly honoured and courted, her statue was led in procession through the fields and bathed in the river to encourage rain, sacrifices and offerings were made to her and so on. Under Christianity the pagan nature of these rituals was glossed over but so important were they to the peasantry that they could not be abolished entirely. Many survived with little fundamental change till the industrialization of agriculture.

The practice of making corn dolls with the last sheaf of corn to be harvested is just one example. The doll was believed to embody the Earth Goddess and was preserved and honoured from one harvest to the next.

Evergreen plants like Ivy were also held in special esteem because they defy the normal round of the seasons. Ivy was even eaten or drunk in a brew during the Dionysian rites of ancient Greece and was believed responsible for the divine frenzy that followed. These rites, also known as Bacchanals, were not quite the self-indulgent orgies they were later portrayed as, but were celebrations of nature's fecundity. The young women wreathed in ivy represented nature spirits and the license permitted was designed to encourage a similar wild abundance in nature.

These festivals were presided over by Dionysus, or Bacchus, but in the background stood his mother Demeter (or Persephone or Semele, it varies in different accounts), because they were a divine and indivisible Mother-Son couple much like Isis and Horus or, for that matter, the Virgin Mary and Jesus. This was one reason Dionysus was so demonized by the early Christian Church. Another is that he also rose from the dead and ascended to heaven.

◁ **Holly and Ivy**
Linda 1994
Pastel and collage 13 x 15in (33 x 38cm)

GAIA

In Ancient Greece and other parts of the Mediterranean, the Great Mother was identified as Gaia, the bountiful earth that nourishes all things. Out of herself she created Uranus, the starry sky. Then taking him for her husband she gave birth to the Titans and giants and ultimately all other creatures, including humans. As a Homeric poem of the 7th Century BC says:

I shall sing of deep-breasted Gaia,
Mother of All, most ancient of beings,
She feeds all creatures that are in the world,
All beasts that walk upon the goodly land
And all that swim the paths of the sea,
And all birds that fly in the sky:
All these are fed of her store.

Gaia has been called by many names, and her story has been told in many different ways, but they all are trying to tell the same tale, that we are the children, first and foremost, of the earth. Later religions may have obscured her role, denied it even, but in the end she cannot be denied. In the end we are all her children and ignore her at our peril. Not because she is vindictive, but one might as well try to deny the existence of gravity, hunger, the ocean tides or winter.

In Greek myth, Uranus was endlessly unfaithful to his wife so finally she encouraged their son Cronos to drive him into exile and take his place. Uranus was banished to the distant heavens where he had little influence on human affairs and so was thereafter largely ignored. Gaia retired too, but of her own choice and only to an extent. She handed over many duties to her daughter Rhea and other goddesses, but continued to be honoured in her own right until the advent of Christianity.

Gaia was seen as the mother of humans as well as gods, and it was to her that both ultimately turned for sanction of their deeds. She presided over marriages, fertility, health and prophecy, and was the ultimate guardian of solemn oaths. Until she handed over to Apollo, it was she who spoke through the Oracle at Delphi, the navel of the world. It was to her that the first fruits of harvest were offered. In form she was represented as a gigantic woman, so large that when making an oath she was able to reach down and touch the River Styx without leaving Olympus.

After succeeding his father Uranus, Cronos married his sister Rhea. They had three daughters, Hestia, Demeter and Hera; and three sons, Hades, Poseidon and Zeus. Sadly Cronos turned out to be as much a disappointment as his father. Having been warned that one of his children would overthrow him, he swallowed them all at birth. In despair Rhea turned to Gaia when due to give birth to Zeus. Gaia whisked her off to the island of Crete and when the child was born she delivered him into the safekeeping of the nymphs of nearby Mt Ida. Rhea meanwhile presented Cronos with a stone wrapped up in swaddling clothes, which he unsuspectingly swallowed instead.

Shielded by the nymphs and suckled by the milk of the marvellous goat Amalthea, Zeus grew to fulfil the prophecy by overthrowing Cronos, forcing

him to vomit up all the children he had swallowed and then imprisoning him underground in distant Thule. The rock Cronos had swallowed in error was set up at Delphi as a reminder of this. When Amalthea died, Zeus set her in the heavens as the constellation Capricorn and wore her hide as a protective cloak. Later he gave it to Athene as a cover for her shield. One of Amalthea's horns (or perhaps the only one) was given to the nymphs in gratitude and was called the Cornucopia, or Horn of Plenty, because it provided as much food or drink as anyone could consume.

Zeus and Hera eventually replaced their parents to rule over the more familiar gods of Mount Olympus, who were later adopted by the Romans and remain known to us through the part they play in astrology. Gaia slipped into the background but has lately enjoyed a revival as a kind of non-sectarian Earth Goddess and embodiment of the spirit of the Green movement. But it is worth remembering that Gaia also represents the moon and some stars.

The ancient Greeks had many different versions of the Creation myth but most agree on what we have said about Gaia so far. Where they disagree is on what came before, and how exactly she arose from Chaos and Night. Some say Night or Nyx gave birth to a mystical egg from which hatched Love or Eros whose bright arrows sparked the universe into being. Then come several other proto-deities before the story picks up with Gaia. In other accounts Gaia herself seems to be the mystical egg floating upon the dim waters, till she stirred and gave birth to Uranus and all the rest followed.

Either way Gaia is Mother of the Sky as well as the Earth, so once Creation was set in motion she became the Tree of Life that unites the two. This is hinted at in the legend of the Phoenix which every five hundred years returns to nest and be reborn amid flames in the crown of a palm tree in Arabia, the palm being how people in the Middle East envisioned the Tree of Life.

The Pelasgians, who inhabited Greece before the Hellenes, had a simpler account. To them Gaia was known as Eurynome, Goddess of All Things. Eurynome emerged from Chaos and wanted to dance, but found nowhere to plant her feet. So she divided the sea from the sky and danced alone on the surface of the slow waves. Dancing towards the south, she stirred a wind behind her. Feeling it touch her back, she turned and caught it in her hands, whereupon the wind became the great serpent Ophion with whom she now danced in a heat of passion till she felt new life stirring in her womb.

Taking the form of a dove, Eurynome flew over the waves and then laid an egg on the waters. Ophion coiled himself around the egg at her bidding and split it in two, whereupon out tumbled the sun, moon and stars, and the earth ready formed. Eurynome and Ophion settled on Mount Olympus at the centre of the world, but Ophion boasted so much that he was the originator of all things that Eurynome finally lost patience and banished him to a pit deep under the earth. Then she created seven divine couples to rule the seven planets, which were the Titans familiar to us from other accounts.

IMBOLC

△ **Winter**
Linda 1994
Oils 16 x 16in (41 x 41cm)

This is the ancient Celtic festival of Brigid celebrated on the 1st or 2nd February when winter seems at its bleakest but is in fact giving way to spring. 'Imbolc' means literally 'in the womb' because life is now stirring invisibly within the earth. The days have already been lengthening since the Winter Solstice and although the weather is generally at its coldest now, signs of new life are beginning to show. Another name for the feast is 'Oimelc' meaning 'ewe's milk' because this is the start of the lambing season.

Under Christianity the feast became that of St Brigit, in Ireland at least, and continued with little change. It was also called Candlemas, candles being used to symbolize the glow of life preserved within the frozen earth. At Candlemas all lamps and fires in the house would be lit to encourage the return of life.

Beltane or May Eve marks the end of spring and the beginning of summer. It is another fire festival and at one time cattle were driven through Beltane bonfires to purify them of any lingering malaises. Along with Halloween it is one of the ancient celebrations that has survived best into modern times. Even at its strongest the Church could do little in rural societies beyond tutting in disapproval and turning a blind eye, because May Eve celebrates fertility in the form of sexuality, about which the Church had little positive to say.

This is the time when the landscape seriously begins to change into its summer dress. Flowers and trees burgeon and bloom. The Maypole, representing the Tree of Life, is decked with streamers and made the centerpiece of carefree celebrations of life .

BELTANE

△ **Spring**
Linda 1993
Oils 16 x 16in (41 x 41cm)

LUGHNASAD

The first of August is an early harvest festival, a celebration of the first fruits of the earth. It stands at the opposite pole of the year from Brigid's Night and to the ancient Celts was a commemoration of the death and rebirth of Brigid's consort Lugh, the Celtic sun god. With the coming of Christianity the festival was partially preserved in the many traditions and songs about John Barleycorn, who dies and is reborn as soul-cheering ale.

In Medieval times the festival became known as Lammas, or Loaf Mass because the corn had usually just been harvested and could be ground by the miller and baked into bread. Corn dolls were made, reminders of Brigid or the Earth Mother who presided over the old celebrations, and this was a day when couples could engage in trial marriages lasting a year and a day, at the end of which they could decide whether or not to call in the priest and make it official.

Samaine, better known to us as Halloween, marked for the ancient Celts the transition from the old year to the new, just as for them time was measured in 'nights' rather than 'days', as reflected in the surviving term 'fortnight'. It is also the scariest night of the year because at Samaine the gates between the worlds are thrown open and all kinds of ghosts and monsters are set free to walk abroad. This is when the fairy folk in Celtic lands moved from their summer to their winter residences and the only safe course for humans was to gather in large numbers around bonfires, or bolt the door and pull the bedclothes tight over their heads.

It is a great time for fortune telling, because the veil between the worlds is so thin. This is the time for single people to try one of the many charms for determining who their future partner will be.

SAMAINE

△ **Autumn**
Linda 1992
Oils 16 x 16in (40 x 40cm)

DEMETER

Demeter was one of the three daughters of Cronos and Rhea. She took no part in the great war in which the Titans were overthrown, but afterwards became one of the six great goddesses of Olympus, along with Hera (Juno), Athene (Minerva), Artemis (Diana), Hestia (Vesta) and Aphrodite (Venus). Their more familiar Roman names are given in brackets. Demeter herself was known to them as Ceres, from which we get the word 'cereal'.

Gaia and her successor Rhea represented the earth itself whereas Demeter represented agriculture, the tilled and tamed earth. She was the goddess of crops. She is often portrayed holding sheaves of corn, poppies and snakes. In Arcadia she was sometimes represented with a horse's head surrounded by serpents and wild beasts, holding a dolphin in one hand and a dove in the other. The ancient Celts revered her as Epona, the white mare, and carved her likeness into the hills. Besides agriculture, Demeter was seen as the dispenser of laws, and hence civilization; and of oracles, a

function she shared with Gaia.

Poseidon, the sea-god, fell in love with Demeter but she refused his advances. She fled to Arcadia and took on the form of a mare to escape him. But he chased her along the river Styx, found her and, taking the shape of a stallion, fathered on her the wild horse Arion, who had the the power of speech. Furious at this violation, Demeter cursed the River Styx, which thereafter became the River of Death. She also left Olympus and hid herself in a cave until Zeus came to coax her back.

Then Zeus himself fell in love with her. When she refused him he assumed the form of a bull and took her by force. From this union came the beautiful Kore, who delighted in flowers and whose tale is inseparable from Demeter's.

One day when Kore was picking flowers, the ground suddenly opened and she was seized by Hades, god of the underworld, who carried her off in a chariot down to his dreary kingdom. Demeter heard Kore cry but could find no trace of her daughter. She searched far and wide till finally Helios, the sun god who sees everything, told her what had happened. Helios said also that Zeus was to blame because he had promised Kore to Hades as a bride. Once again Demeter withdrew from Olympus and wandered the world in mourning clothes and the guise of a common mortal.

In Eleusis she was taken in by the kindly King Celeus and his family and given charge of Celeus' baby son, who blossomed marvellously under her care. She was grooming him in fact for immortality, feeding him only on ambrosia and baptising him each night with fire. This ended when her divinity was accidentally revealed. But when the time came to leave she repaid their kindness by teaching Celeus' eldest son Triptolemus the art of ploughing, sowing corn and reaping the harvest, which is how agriculture came to Greece and the world.

Also in her wanderings Demeter introduced the cultivation of the olive tree. But finally, unable to overcome grief at the loss of her daughter, she withdrew all her blessings from the earth and unending cold and famine gripped the world. All the gods in turn came to plead with her but Demeter refused to let the earth bear fruit until she saw her daughter again. Finally Zeus commanded Hades to free Kore, who by now was known as Persephone or Proserpine, which means 'she who destroys light'. Hades had no choice but to agree, but first he tempted Persephone to eat a few pomegranate seeds. This doubly bound her to him because the seed-filled pomegranate is a symbol of marriage, and anyone who tastes the food of the underworld is condemned to remain there.

When Demeter heard of this she was overcome with grief and fury. Afraid of her revenge, Zeus and Rhea forged a compromise by which Persephone would spend just one third of the year in the underworld with her husband and the rest on the surface. To this Demeter agreed and allowed the earth to bear fruit again for as long as Persephone was away from Hades. Thus did the seasons come into being.

Demeter then consented to return to Olympus and forget her grievances, and before leaving she intitiated humans into her mysteries. The tale of Kore or Persephone was commemorated every year in ancient Greece with two great festivals, one in October to mark her departure into the underworld and the other in February marking her return. Every five years in September there

△ **Persephone**
Roger 1998
Pen and Ink (actual size)

◁ **Poppies**
Linda 1998
Oils 6 x 6in (15 x 15cm)

was held the greatest festival of all, in Athens and Eleusis, marked by the sacrifice of pigs. Cows, wine, fruit and milk were also offered up to her and the initiated celebrated her mysteries. Which, however, largely remain mysteries because they were transmitted orally and with strict injunctions of secrecy. It is known however that they concentrated on death and rebirth, both in nature and humans.

At the centre of the ritual was a reaped ear of corn, in whose annual rebirth was seen a pattern for human reincarnation. There is believed to be a close parallel between the Eleusinian mysteries and those of Isis and Osiris in Egypt, Aphrodite and Adonis in Syria and Cybele and Attis in Phrygia; except that in those cases it is a male corn god that gets lost in the Underworld.

At Eleusis Demeter continued to be honoured right up to the nineteenth century when a visiting English scholar ran off with her great statue and presented it to Cambridge University.

THE CORN MOTHER

Demeter is often seen as the earth and Persephone as the corn that springs from it; but it is more likely that as mother and daughter they are just two aspects of the same deity representing the old crop and the new, and the continuity between them. Under other names and guises Demeter, as the Corn Mother, was worshipped from the Mediterranean right up to the frozen wastes of northern Europe, and as a folk custom this continued long after the arrival of Christianity. In Germany they used to say 'The Corn Mother is coming' when the wind rippled through a field of wheat or barley; and children tempted to play in the field, or pick the corn-flowers or poppies were warned that the Corn Mother would get them if they did.

Over wide areas of northern Europe it was once believed that the Corn Mother was present in the last sheaf of corn left in a field, so this was made into a doll and carried home in style on a wagon. A wreath was made of flowers and the finest ears of corn and worn as a crown by the prettiest maid in the village, who would then present it to the local squire or landlord. The Corn Mother doll presided over the harvest celebrations, then was carried to the barn to watch over the threshing and guard the harvest against mice and other thieves. At Christmas she was moved to the cattle sheds to foster the beasts' fertility. Then at Easter a young girl was chosen to pick the seeds out of the doll and scatter them among the new corn growing in the fields to encourage its growth.

Some or all of these customs, or variations on them, are still to be found in some rural areas, particularly in Scandinavia; and besides barley and wheat they apply also to flax, oats, rye and all similar crops. Sometimes the effigy is called the Old Woman or the Grandmother or even the Great Mother and there are often contests among unmarried youngsters to gain her special favour in finding them a partner.

In the west of Scotland the corn doll was called the Old Wife (Cailleach) and there was great competition NOT to be the one to take her home because it was believed that entertaining the Corn Mother for the winter could drain the energy of a farm, no matter how much good it did for the neighbours. The

honour usually went to the slowest reaper in the village or island. When the time came to sow the fields next year, all the other farmers came for a part of the doll which they fed to their plough horses, or scattered about their fields to ensure a good crop.

Most commonly the spirit captured in the last sheaf of corn was considered mature or elderly but in some regions such as eastern Scotland she was called the Corn Maiden and in others the Corn Bride. In some parts of Scotland both a Maiden and Mother were made, the Maiden being kept by the farmer on whose land she grew and the Mother being presented to the neighbour who was last to finish the harvest. With which we return to Demeter and Persephone, whose drama it is that the farmers were unconsciously celebrating.

Details of the rites surrounding corn dolls vary but what is more remarkable is how much they had in common right across Europe and how stubbornly they persisted into the nineteenth and even the twentieth century. Details varied but the general drift of the festivities was the same. One way or another the idea was to catch and nurture the spirit of the crop from one year to the next so that it should thrive through all the vagaries of weather, pestilence and all the other uncertainties of the farmer's life.

Earth Border
Linda
Oils (actual size)

Autumn Jewellery and Collage
Linda 1998

4 ELEMENT AIR

The elements Air and Fire tend to be dominated by male deities, but the goddesses are there if you look hard enough. In the most patriarchal mythologies there are traces of an older order where things were very different. In Greek mythology the Titans were arranged in divine couples in which there are strong echoes of a time when the female in most couples was the dominant partner. When the Titans were overthrown Zeus presided over the new order and the many tales of his arguments with his wife Hera have been read as reflecting backlashes from the old goddess cults defending their dignity.

Pagan Greek mythology is much less patriarchal than some, however, and in the portraits it draws of Hera, Artemis, Aphrodite, Demeter and so on we get a very lively impression of the faces of the goddess in her ascendance. In the way they are paired with gods we get a clear picture of which god took over which goddess' place in the hierarchy. For most constellations of divine activity there is basically a male-female couple, either of whom can emerge to the forefront depending on the cultural mood of the time.

So it is not that surprising that the sky and the earth, say, should have different genders in different cultures. Just as there is a lingering memory in the West of the Man in the Moon as opposed to the more common Woman, so for most gods there is a corresponding goddess who once stood in his place, and vice versa. Often the stories remain the same with just the gender and name of the principal actors changed. Then sometimes, as in Egypt, many original features of the matriarchal religion survived unchanged even after the balance of power had shifted towards the male.

◁ **Frost**
Linda 1994
Oils 8 x 12in (20 x 30cm)

Nut

Nut in Egyptian mythology is the personification of the vault of heaven who touches the earth only with her fingers and toes. Her starry belly is the night sky. Geb, the earth, is masculine and is her twin brother and husband.

According to the most ancient papyri all that existed in the beginning was Nun, a boundless primaeval water shrouded in darkness. Finally the spirit of the water felt the urge of creation, uttered its own secret name and emerged into being within a lotus that floated on the water. Known as Khepera or Atum, he then formed an egg from which sprang Ra, the shining sun, the new embodiment of his own divine spirit. The names Khepera and Atum were afterwards applied to the rising and setting suns.

Out of himself Ra brought forth Shu and Tefnut, the original divine couple. Shu was god of the atmosphere and is always depicted in human form. Tefnut, his consort, was goddess of the dew and rain and was shown as a lioness, or a

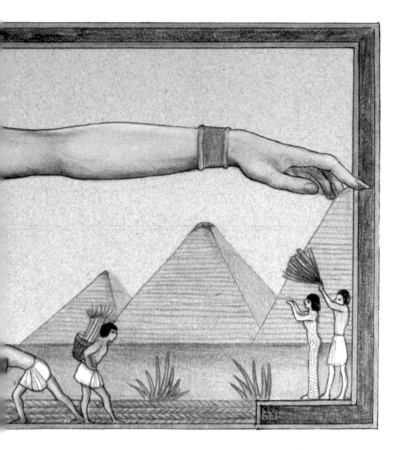

human with a lioness head. Each morning she welcomes the newborn sun rising in the east. Tefnut gave birth to Geb and Nut, the earth and sky who were inseparably entwined until on Ra's orders Shu forced them apart to make the world as we know it. Some say that Geb and Nut married against Ra's wishes and that is why they were separated. Geb has mourned this ever since.

Nut in due course gave birth simultaneously to Isis and Osiris, Nepthys and Set, creating the pantheon that was to dominate Egyptian religion for thousands of years.

The sun had many names in ancient Egypt besides Ra and was conceived of in many ways that are now rather confusing. Principally he was seen as the child of Nut (as well as being her grandparent), born anew from her each day and growing to old age by the end of his ride across the sky in a ship. During the night he had to traverse the underworld to be born again. At the same time he was pictured as a divine scarab beetle rolling the disc of the sun across the sky or, along with the moon, one of the eyes of a great celestial hawk.

Originally Ra lived and ruled on earth at Heliopolis, but finally he grew old and weary of this existence. At his request Nut transformed herself into a cow and elevated him to heaven where he began the course he has followed ever since. Because of this service Nut is often pictured as a cow whose four legs are the pillars of the sky. She is a protectress of the dead and is often portrayed

Nut
Linda 1997
Pastel and ink 10 x 16 1/2 in (25 x 42cm)

Raki and Papa

The Egyptians saw the sky as female and the earth as male, but more commonly it is the other way round. In India there circulated similar myths of the separation of sky and earth, but their genders are reversed; the earth is the wife, the sky is the husband and the atmosphere (equivalent of Shu) holds them apart.

The Maori of New Zealand tell the story this way: Raki, the god of heaven, and Papa, the earth goddess, were the parents of all living things. At that time they were locked in intimate embrace and darkness lay over all things. Finally their children grew weary of the continual gloom. Also they could hardly move because of being crushed between their parents, and there was no room for things to grow. So they gathered in conference to decide what to do. Some said they must kill Raki and Papa but Tane-mahuta, god of the forests and all who dwell in them, stood forth and cried out: 'No, it is better to tear them apart, to let the heaven stand high above us and the earth beneath our feet. Let Raki become a stranger to us, but let Papa lie close and be our nursing mother.'

Four other gods agreed to this proposal. The first to try separating Raki and Papa was Rongo-matane, god of agriculture. Next came Tangaroa, god of fish and reptiles. Then Haumia, god of wild fruits, and Tu-matauenga, god of human heroes, tried their hands and all failed. Then Tane-mahuta arose and placed himself between his parents. He heaved with all his might but Raki and Papa clung close and resisted him. Then Tane stood on his head and thrust the sky up with his feet, pushing like a tree against the sky. Raki and Papa groaned and shrieked and were slowly torn from each others arms.

'Why are you killing us, your mother and father?' they cried.

But Tane only pressed all the harder with his feet and forced Raki high above the earth. Then seeing that they were beaten, Raki said sadly to his wife 'O Papa, there you must remain but in the eighth month I will weep for you as a token of my love.' This was the origin of dew and rain.

Then Raki said: 'O my love, in winter I will sigh for you,' and this was the origin of snow and ice.

Papa replied: 'O Raki, go if you must, and in summer I too will lament for you!' This was the origin of mist.

Then they were separated and Tane raised high mountains to keep them apart, and for the first time lightness and dark were made manifest. Tane thus became the god of light, the sun, parent of the Dawn Maid, fertilizer of the earth and renewer of the light of Hina, the moon. He also set the stars in their places, the fixed and the moving ones; in particular Ao-tahi, the Morning Star. Some Maori say that Raki and Papa's grief later turned to bitterness and loathing, helped perhaps by this curse from the goddess Whai-tiri:

> *Rough be their skin, so changed by dread*
> *As bramble and nettle, loathsome to touch.*
> *So change for each other their love into hate,*
> *With dire enchantments, O sever them, gods!*
> *Fill their days with disgust for each other*
> *Engulf them in floods, in ocean and sea.*

With dire enchantments, O sever them, gods!
Let love and yearning for each other become hate,
Nor affection nor love of the past live again.

So sky and earth were separated and light came into the Maori world, but so did other unforseen things. Violence breeds violence, and to avenge the hurt done to Raki and Papa, the god of storms and tempests Tawhiri turned on the others with whirlwinds and thunder and lightning. Riding in the midst of a hurricane he scattered the other gods before him. Then they regrouped and took sides, some siding with Tawhiri and some with Tane, and to a greater or lesser degree they have been at war ever since.

Thus did evil come into the world along with light. Man, beasts and birds went to war with each other, and even amongst themselves, and death walked abroad for the first time.

Elsewhere in the Pacific similar tales were told and often the gods even have the same names; particularly Tangaroa, god of the ocean, whose moods so dominate the lives of Pacific islanders. In New Zealand Tangaroa is just one of six more or less equal divinities but elsewhere he is honoured as the supreme creator. In carvings he is often shown as being covered in tiny gods or humans who seem to be bursting from his flesh fully formed. In some parts of Polynesia Tangaroa is credited with having created a cosmic egg from which sprang humanity and all other creatures. In Samoa his daughter Tuli is said to have done this.

Hina, the moon, is also widely known under the same name as a patron of women's activities. But unsurprisingly, given the scattered nature of Oceania, on some islands they explain things totally differently. On the island of Nauru in Micronesia they say the world came about this way: In the beginning there was nothing but the dim sea, above which floated the Old-Spider. One day the Old-Spider found a giant clam shell floating on the waters. She took it up and tapped it. It sounded hollow and empty, so she chanted a spell and the two halves of the shell opened a little.

Old-Spider slipped inside and found it very dark because the sun and moon did not then exist. Then she found she could not stand up because the shell was too cramped. Hunting around in the dark she found two snails, one of which she persuaded to open the shell a little. This it did and was made into the moon. By the moon's light Old-Spider saw a big worm which she persuaded to open the shell a bit more. The worm's sweat as it forced the shells apart gathered in the lower half to form the ocean. Then the worm raised the upper shell very high till it became the sky. The worm then died of exhaustion and from the second snail Old-Spider created the sun.

The creation of islands in the Pacific is commonly attributed to the hero god Maui who hauled them up like fish from the deep. Maui also championed humans against the gods and stole fire for them from heaven. Where islands were not supposed to have been fished out of the deep, many other explanations are offered: they are rocks thrown by the gods, eggs dropped by divine birds, or sometimes they were created by the churnings of a great serpent from the ocean depths.

USHAS

Hail, gentle Dawn! mild blushing goddess, hail!
Rejoiced I see thy purple mantle spread
O'er half the skies: gems pave thy radiant way,
And orient pearls from every shrub depend.

The peculiarly fresh and optimistic beauty of the bright dawn, the almost tangible uplift of cheer provoked by the sun's first clear rays glancing out of the east, is personified in most mythologies by a youthful goddess. In ancient Greece this was Aurora, or Eos, younger sister of the sun and moon. Sometimes in her saffron robes she appears in the east riding Pegasus or a chariot drawn by two white steeds.

Morning dew comes from the tears Aurora still sheds for her son Memnon, slain by Achilles in the Battle of Troy. Memnon's father was the mortal Tithonius with whom Aurora fell so deeply in love she asked Zeus to grant him immortality. Zeus did so but she had neglected to ask that he also be forever young, then had to suffer watching Tithonius wither to a grotesque husk of his handsome youth. Finally the gods took pity and turned him into a cicada.

In Slav myth it is Zorya who, with the aid of the Morning Star, opens the gates of the celestial palace for the sun's white horses at daybreak and sets them on their course. She and her sisters Evening and Midnight also have charge of the dog linked by a chain to the constellation of the Little Bear. When the chain breaks it will be the end of the universe, so this is no minor duty.

In Hindu mythology the goddess of the dawn is Ushas, who is the daughter of Heaven and sister of Night. She rides a shining chariot drawn by saffron horses or heavenly cows and is born anew each day. Confident in her ever-youthful beauty, she drives the night away with careless displays of her charms. She wakes the righteous with a smile to the challenges of the day but lets the wicked sleep so that opportunities will pass them by. To escape the incestuous advances of her father Prajapati she took on the form of a gazelle, which animal then became sacred to her.

Ushas is the first of all to wake,
She yokes her chariot from above the rising sun,
Comes gloriously unto men on many wheels,
And tramples over passing night.

Mighty Goddess, bringer of the light,
Spying every thing from Heaven's height,
Ever youthful, all reviving Dawn,
To every invocation comes She first.

Ushas, daughter born of Heaven,
Dawn on us with Thy riches, spreading light,
Dawn on us with abundance of food,
Delightful Goddess, dawn upon us with wealth.

◁ **Ushas**
Linda 1998
Oils and collage 8 x 12in (21 x 30cm)

The Valkyries

The Valkyries of Teutonic myth are the dispensers of justice and fortune in battle. Visible only to those about to die, they ride above the battlefield on flying steeds in full armour and legendary breastplates, fire streaming from their spears. A strange light flickers around them that is said to be the Aurora Borealis, or Northern Lights.

The name 'Valkyrie' means in Norse 'She who chooses the slain', and of those who die in battle it is the Valkyries who decide which should join the heroes' feast in Valhalla, Odin's palace in Asgard beyond the rainbow bridge where every day the guests feast and fight, are miraculously cured of their wounds and go back to feasting again. The frame of this hall is made of vast spears, the roof is tiled with glittering shields and the walls hung with shining swords and armour which blaze in reflection of the leaping fire in the midst of the tables.

Odin calls all the greatest warriors to his feast because he knows that one day he faces a great battle with the giants. So from his throne in Valhalla he is forever scanning the earth for new champions, and listening to the news of his ravens who every day scour our world, Midgard, for gossip that may interest him. The Valkyrie are Odin's guards and handmaidens, waiting upon him and his guests at the feast. But when he spies a battle looming, Odin despatches them down into Midgard to oversee it and bring new champions to him.

The Valkyries, usually acting on Odin's orders, also decide which side should win the battle and often join in personally with sword and spear to ensure the outcome. Other weapons they use are inspiration, madness, courage and cowardice, so the most vital boon a warrior can carry into battle is their favour.

They also sometimes visit the world as swan-maidens (though not all swan-maidens are Valkyries). If they wish, they can slip off their plumage and step out as beautiful young women, and this they often do to bathe in isolated pools and streams. In the old days it was every warrior's dream to come upon them like this and lay hands on their feathered cloaks, because then they were obliged to serve him.

This is how Brunhilde and eight of her sisters fall into the power of King Agnar in Wagner's opera. Agnar hides their magic cloaks under an oak tree and forces Brunhilde to help him in a war he is engaged in. The trouble is that Odin has already decided that Agnar should lose the battle. When it turns out otherwise, Odin is furious with Brunhilde, strips her of her Valkyrie powers and bans her from returning to Asgard. Then he pricks her with a magic thorn that casts her into a deep sleep, and raises a wall of fire around her that none but the greatest of heroes can pass.

There are many tales of Valkyries and other swan-maidens who have married humans and lived happily with them, at least for a while. Queen of them all is Freya, or Freyja, the Teutonic goddess of spring, music, flowers and love. She is the northern counterpart of Venus and sister to Frey, the god of rain, sunshine and all the fruits of the earth.

Freya

When Thor's enchanted hammer was stolen by a giant, Freya lent her feathered cloak to wily Loki so he could fly off to Jotunheim, the giants' realm, in search of it. Loki learned that the giant Thrym had buried the hammer at a depth of eight fathoms and would not return it unless Freya agreed to become his wife. When Loki returned with this message and the gods tried to persuade Freya to go along with it, she was so outraged her neck swelled up till it burst her golden necklace. So instead, Thor dressed himself up in women's clothing, added Freya's necklace and a heavy bridal veil and set off for Jotunheim himself, accompanied by Loki disguised as a servant.

When it was announced at Thrym's castle that Freya had come to be his bride, the giant laid on a great wedding feast. He was then slightly astonished when his bride consumed an entire ox, eight salmon and countless side dishes (Thor had a famous appetite). But Loki quickly said that Freya had not eaten for a week because she had been so excited by the prospect of this marriage. Thrym was reassured and began to get excited again himself at the prospect of bedding down that night with the goddess of love. Then he lifted her veil to snatch a kiss and was so startled by the fierce visage and flashing eyes he met that he leaped away. Again Loki soothed him, saying that Freya's passions had been so inflamed by Thrym's proposal that she had been unable to sleep for a week and was burning up with desire.

Thrym grew impatient again to get the formalities over with, so he sent for Thor's hammer, upon which they would pledge their union. (Aside from being the greatest of warriors, Thor was the patron and guarantor of oaths. All the greatest pledges in Asgard were made over his enchanted hammer.) The hammer was brought from hiding and placed, according to the custom, on the bride's knees. With a joyful shout Thor sprang up with it and proceeded to despatch Thrym and all his followers to the Underworld.

Freya, the goddess of love, is sometimes distinguished from Odin's wife, Frija or Frigg, but more often they seem to be the same. She is the first Valkyrie and their queen. Often like the rest she will wait on Odin's guests, but also she can take her pick of the heroes for her own feast in the palace of Folkvang.

Both Freya and Odin indulge in many extramarital affaires and occasionally provoke each other to jealous fury because of it, but neither seems willing or able to curb their own appetites. And although Freya refused to lie with the giant Thrym, she is not always so choosy.

Near her palace in a cave once lived four dwarves who were wonderful jewellers. Passing by one day, Freya fell in love with a dazzling golden necklace they had made. She offered any amount of gold and silver for it, but the dwarves only laughed and said they already had all the metals they could wish for. But they would let her have it if she agreed to spend a night with each of them, which is how she bought her necklace. Odin was furious when he found out. He persuaded Loki to steal the necklace and, after a heated argument when Freya came to reclaim it, extracted various promises and penances before he would give it back.

was the favourite handmaid of Hera, queen of the heavenly court on Mt Olympus. She kept guard at the foot of Hera's throne, drew her bath, laid out her clothes and carried out all the other duties of a handmaid. She was also Hera's messenger, a feminine counterpart to Hermes (Mercury) and had shimmering wings to speed her flight. Homer calls her 'fleet Iris of the Whirlwind Feet' and she travels so fast that all we usually see is the trail of her multicoloured passage across the sky.

In one hand Iris carries the caduceus, the herald's wand entwined by two snakes symbolizing the reconciliation of opposites. None of this may be visible though because Iris often adopts human guise when visiting mortals. She travels through air, sea or underworld with equal ease because, having no enemies, nothing tries to bar her way.

Unless on some stern errand for Hera or Zeus, Iris is helpful and compassionate to all she meets, both human and divine. It was she who finally ended Leto's long and painful labour when giving birth to Artemis and Apollo by fetching the goddess of childbirth, even though it was her mistress Hera who was deliberately detaining that goddess to prolong Leto's suffering. She helped rescue Zeus' golden dog Pandareus from the Underworld. Some say that Eros, or love, was the child of Iris and the wind god Zephyrus, though it is more commonly believed Eros was Aphrodite's child, or was born directly from the World Egg.

Among Iris' duties was that of leading the souls of dead women to the Elysian fields, so Greeks planted the purple Iris flower on women's graves. The Iris flower was dedicated to the goddess because it blooms in all the shades of the rainbow. The iris of the eye was so named for similar reasons.

Iris was connected to the land of the dead in another way. Hesiod's Theogony tells us that: 'when strife and quarrel arise among the deathless gods, and when any one of them who live in the house of Olympus tells a lie, then Zeus sends Iris to bring in a golden jug the great oath of the gods' from far away, the famous cold water which trickles down from a high and beetling rock.

'The oath of the gods' was a draught of water from a spring connected with the gloomy River Styx on the borders of the Underworld. Any deity who breaks an oath toasted with this water must suffer a terrible forfeit. For a year they lie in a trance, unable

IRIS

Like fiery clouds that flush with ruddy glare,
Or Iris gliding through the purple air:
When loosely girt her dazzling mantle flows,
And gainst the sun in arching colours glows.

The ancient Greeks personified the rainbow as the goddess Iris, daughter of the Titans Thaumas and Electra. She was sister to the dreadful Harpies, monstrous hags with birds' bodies, but was as unlike them as possible. Despite their differences, she pleaded for her sisters' lives when the Argonauts threatened to kill them.

Iris herself was sweet and gentle and kind. She

to breathe or eat nectar and ambrosia, but fully aware of their need for it. Then for nine more years they are banished from Olympus and all its delights. 'Such an oath, then, did the gods appoint the eternal and primeval water of Styx to be: and it spouts through a rugged place.'

Iris' main temple was at Delos.

Among the Iroquois and other native Americans the rainbow is considered the wife of the thunder god and one of the attendants of the sun and moon. In west Africa she is considered the benevolent servant of the thunder god who attempts to heal the damage done by her master. They also speak of a Rainbow Snake that encircles the whole world and holds its tail in its mouth like the Midgard Serpent. The Rainbow Snake is kindly and seeks to unite all the warring factions in the world.

Australian Aborigines also say that the rainbow was originally a snake that in the Dream Time lived near a waterhole where all the birds also lived. Rainbow was dazzlingly handsome and was married to Whistle Duck, whose love he had stolen from Bat. Because of this Bat had left the other birds and gone to live in a cave among the hills, where he sulked and brooded on his wrongs and plotted revenge.

Bat decided he would have to kill Rainbow if he was to get Whistle Duck back, so he spent all his time making spears. The trouble was he knew Rainbow was very strong and it would take a very special spear to kill him.

One day when he was out looking for spear tips he spotted the perfect piece of limestone jutting from a rock. He broke it off and hurried back to his cave with it, then spent days sharpening it further and fixing it to a shaft. Finally he tested the point of his spear and cut off his own nose, which is why bats have had flat faces ever since.

However, Bat didn't care about this because he was so delighted at having a weapon at last that might conquer Rainbow. That evening he flew down to the waterhole, hid his spear in the bushes and joined the other birds. They were having a dance, as they did every evening, and were pleased to see Bat again because he was the best dancer of them all.

Rainbow was not happy though. He kept Whistle Duck close beside him under the tree and just glared suspiciously as Bat danced away and seemed to be having the time of his life without a grievance in the world.

Finally everyone grew tired and lay down to sleep. All except Bat who only pretended to. After a while, when all was still, he crept off to the bushes, came back with his spear and threw it as hard as he could at Rainbow as he lay sleeping under his tree. Rainbow woke screaming and thrashing around on the ground. All the birds leaped into the air and scattered in fright, and they have mostly been scattered ever since; except for Whistle Duck who stood by watching her husband's agonies. Rainbow was bleeding badly but, little by little, he dragged himself to the waterhole and rolled in. The blessed water healed him and he has dwelt in its depths ever since.

Just occasionally after rain does he emerge and stretch himself across the sky for our delight. You can still see where the blood ran down his lovely body. And as for Duck, well she spends so much time on or beside the waterhole because that is the closest she can now get to her husband. As for Bat, well his plan failed because of course Whistle Duck did not go back to him and he has hidden himself in caves away from the other birds ever since.

◁ **Iris**
Linda 1998
Watercolour 10 x 7in (25 x 18cm)

5

ELEMENT FIRE

KUPALA

HESTIA

VESTA

FIREWALKERS

PHOENIX

Fire has been worshipped for as long as humans have known of its existence, and continued to be worshipped long after we learned how to kindle it for ourselves and were no longer dependent on chance bolts of lightning. Fire was originally regarded quite naturally as a live spirit, a miracle that if contained and nurtured could drive away the dark and cold and wild beasts all at one go, could make food palatable and bend metals to human design. On top of which, with its endless shifting patterns of light when dancing in the hearth it feeds the imagination, conjuring those dreamy visions of other realities which in the end are the mainspring of all human evolution.

The mastery of fire, or more commonly the stealing of its secrets from the gods, is an episode in most mythologies because of the life-transforming impact it made on our remote ancestors. In Ireland this was commemorated annually in pagan times when at certain of the great annual feasts every fire in the land was extinguished and relit from a central sacred flame such as that of Brigid at Kildare. With the Nyanga people of southern Africa until recently, when a tree was struck by lightning, all the village fires were extinguished and relit from it.

Among the Slavonic peoples Fire was a divinity in itself created by the Sky at the same time as the Sun. In Russia she was seen as the Firebird who occasionally sets alight the trees in which she settles. When people learned to extract fire from wood by friction, they understood it as drawing the latent divine, sap-like essence out of the wood; and trees were filled with this essence because their roots drew it up from the fiery depths of the earth. It is likely that the special reverence held for the oak tree comes from the frequency with which it is struck by lightning.

KUPALA

Like the Irish Brigid, the Slavonic goddess Kupala is associated with both fire and water, but in Kupala's case fire seems slightly the stronger element. The holy fires on Kupala's Night, which falls at the Summer Solstice had the power of cleansing both body and soul, so her followers formed chanting rings around them, circling around and leaping through the flames.

The festival of Kupala was presided over by a straw effigy of the goddess dressed in fine robes and adorned with flowers, jewellery and ribbons. This was seated under a birch tree which had been ceremonially chosen by a procession of women through the forest. When the right tree was found, they felled it and carried it by cart back to the festival ground. There all but the crown of top branches were trimmed off, it was set upright in a hole in the ground and decorated with garlands of flowers and ribbons. All this work was done by women, men were not permitted to touch the goddess' tree. Sacrifices and offerings were made before her enthroned effigy under it.

Trees, herbs and flowers were sacred to Kupala. The day of her festival was particularly propitious for finding rare medicinal or magic herbs, such as 'tear-weed' or purple loose-strife whose root bestowed power over evil spirits. They could be exorcised with this formula:

> *'Tear-weed, tear-weed, who has wept so long in vain.*
> *May your tears not flow into the open field,*
> *Or your sobs drift away over the ocean.*
> *But banish wicked demons and witches.*
> *Drown them in your tears if they resist.*
> *Engulf them in pits and precipices if they flee.*
> *May my words be binding for age upon century!'*

At sunset the goddess' effigy was cast into the festival bonfire or set adrift on a stream. Then came the hunt for Kupala's Fern, the most sacred herb of all. It was believed to produce a single flower just once a year at midnight on Kupala's Night. This flower had almost unlimited powers. To the lucky finder it granted power over demons, revealed the whereabouts of buried treasure and attracted all the kinds of good fortune that can be imagined.

To gather this rare flower one had to be in the forest among the ferns at midnight, which in itself takes a certain courage because on Kupala's Night trees gain the power to move about and converse among themselves in a strange, ancient tongue. Then with luck one might see a glowing bud growing rapidly up the length of a fern and burst at midnight into a flame so bright you must shield your eyes. Then you must trace a magic circle around the blazing flower because it is guarded by devils who will try anything to prevent it being picked. They will assume all kinds of monstrous or pitiful forms which must all be ignored, keeping within the magic circle. Anyone who replies to the demons or even so much as looks at them is lost forever. But if the flower is plucked, the demons will scatter in dismay and the bearer can stroll home safely, fully understanding the language of the trees and many other secret things.

◁ **Cypress** (detail)
Roger 1998
Oils 15 x 36in (38 x 91cm)

Hestia

Hestia, in the high dwellings of all,
Both deathless gods and men who walk upon earth,
You have gained everlasting abode and highest honour:
Glorious is your portion and your right.
For without you mortals hold no banquet
Where one does not duly pour sweet wine
In offering to Hestia, both first and last.

The goddess of domestic and public fires in ancient Greece was Hestia, known as Vesta to the Romans, whose Vestal Virgins have conjured idle erotic fantasies among males ever since.

Hestia was the eldest daughter of Rhea and Cronus, and hence granddaughter of Gaia. Along with Hera and Demeter she formed the highest trinity of goddesses on Mt Olympus. Next to Gaia she was the most honoured of them all. The first and last fruits or libations were always offered to her and on Olympus her place was at the centre of the banquet. These honours recognized the importance of fire to civilization. She is also said to have built the first house.

Along with Artemis and Athene, Hestia was one of the immortal virgins. It is said this came about when in the early days on Mt Olympus, Poseidon and Apollo both sought her hand in marriage. Unable to cause grief to either, she took a vow of eternal chastity, earning Zeus' eternal gratitude because of the dispute she thus avoided. Apollo seems to have borne no grudge because his temples and Hestia's were later often adjoined.

As an eternal virgin Hestia is a guardian of stability, the complete opposite of sweet, mischievous, trouble-stirring Aphrodite. As patroness of the domestic hearth, which is her altar, she promotes harmony within the family that gathers around it, and protects them against dangers from outside. In the old days when family members moved out they would take some of the home fire with them to the new place to ensure spiritual continuity and future ties.

Each town and village in ancient Greece also had a communal flame dedicated to Hestia, so she thus also cared for the safety and peace of the community as a whole and, beyond that, the nation. When new towns and cities were established abroad, fire was carried carefully to them from the home town. The greatest of Hestia's temples was at Delphi, the navel of the world, and sacrifices there were aimed to promote harmony and peace through all humanity. The word 'hestia' means simply 'hearth' in Greek and applies equally to the goddess and her altars.

Because half the tales of the ancient Greek goddesses and gods are basically scandalous, Hestia plays little part in them. On one occasion the god Priapus attempted to ravish her as she and the other immortals lay sleeping after a forest feast. She was woken in time by the braying of an ass and sent Priapus comically packing; but few other adventures are on record.

Hestia was the gentle one the other deities turned to for comfort when licking their wounds and piecing their lives back together after an adventure. She was much loved, honoured and appreciated but was not a very active force in the divine drama. Sculptures show her either sitting or standing, but motionless. She is the still point at the centre of tumultuous creation, rarely taking sides in disputes but looking instead for the point of agreement.

Vesta

As with most of their principal deities, the Romans adopted Hestia and merged her with their own goddess Vesta, whose beauty outshone even that of Venus. To the very early Romans Vesta was a goddess of earth as well as fire, but this attribute faded along with other distinctions between them. She remained, though, a patroness of fertility despite being a virgin because of her domestic concerns. Like the huntress Diana she was a caring midwife without ever wanting to partake of the mysteries of birth herself. Families repaid her by offering up to her the first portions of any food or drink partaken in the house. She shared her hearth willingly with other household deities such as the Lares and Penates, gods of household goods and the larder.

The public cult of Vesta in Rome was said to have been founded by Romulus himself, who along with his twin brother was the son of a Vestal Virgin who claimed to have been made pregnant by Mars himself, appropriately enough, given the course of Roman history. Romulus (or possibly his successor Numa Pompilius) built a great circular temple to Vesta in the Roman Forum where celebrations were held throughout the year save for the months of January and November.

Similar circular temples were built throughout the growing Roman Empire and Vesta was equally honoured throughout until the end of paganism. Her chief festival was the Vestalia which began on the seventh day of June and lasted a week. Normally her sanctuary could be visited only by the Vestal Virgins who tended the holy flame, but at Vestalia any mother could visit the goddess with offerings of food and drink. As in the home, she shared her sanctuary with the Lares and Penates when their responsibilities spread beyond individual households. Likenesses of the goddess generally show her veiled.

There were originally only two Vestal Virgins but their number was later increased to four and then six. Their dress was that of Roman brides and very similar to that of later Christian nuns. Vestal Virgins were chosen by lot from among the leading Roman families and entered service before the age of ten. For the next ten years they were instructed in their duties. For the following ten they practised in the temple, and for the final decade they trained their successors. After this they were permitted to retire to normal life if they chose.

Absolute chastity was required of the Vestals, in contrast with the temple 'virgins' of many other goddesses who often slept with supplicants for ritual purposes on the command of their mistress. They were virgins only in the sense that no man took precedence over their goddess.

With Vestal Virgins any straying from the straight and narrow was punished by a hideously unpleasant death. In eleven centuries this is said to have happened only twenty times. One of the accused proved her innocence by succeeding in carrying water from the Tiber in a sieve. Vestals who let the flame go out were punished by whipping and the flame had to be rekindled by focussing the rays of the sun through a crystal. The only time the flame was permitted to go out was at the start of the year when it was ceremonially extinguished and rekindled in the primordial way with fire-sticks. Among the trades, Vesta was the particular patron of bakers.

△ **Firewalkers**
Linda 1987
Oils 7 x 7in (18 x 18cm)

FIREWALKERS

Firewalking is one way the element has been revered down the ages, and it is still a common feature of religious ceremonial in many parts of the world. In ancient Italy the goddess Feronia, whose shrine was at the foot of Mt Soracte not far from Rome, was honoured in this way. At her festival which attracted vast crowds a great fire of pine wood was built, which men from selected local families would walk across barefoot. In return for this they were exempted from military service and all public duties by the Roman senate.

This custom is mentioned in Virgil's Aeneid but there the deity honoured is said to be Apollo. Possibly, as at Delphi, his temple and the fire-goddess' were adjoining.

Today ceremonial firewalking can be witnessed in India, Japan, China, Africa, Tibet, Sri Lanka, Thailand and many other places, usually as part of some religious festival. Generally men are the main participants but women also take part and in Bali even the children join in.

Amongst Hindus firewalking is the culmination of the Theemithi festival which re-enacts events from the epic Mahabharata. Heroine of this tale is the goddess Draupadi, who was an incarnation of Lakshmi, goddess of prosperity and good fortune and wife of Vishnu. Often Lakshmi is depicted with an elephant's head, but she was also the epitome of feminine beauty.

The Mahabharata tells the story of the struggle for supremacy between the Pandava and Kurava families. The Pandavas are ruled by five brothers who share Draupadi as a wife (or possibly she is only married to Arjuna, the eldest). One day they rashly fall to gambling with the rival Kuravas and manage to lose not only their kingdom but Draupadi as well. For thirteen years, according to the terms of the wager, the Pandavas wander in exile. But when they return to claim back what is theirs, the Kuravas refuse to give it up. The Battle of Kurushetra follows in which the Pandavas are victorious and their enemies are all slain.

Seeing the bodies of her abductors, Draupadi combs her hair for the first time in thirteen years, ever since the Kuravas tried to violate her honour. But there are those who doubt she could have preserved it for so long, so to prove her virtue Draupadi ordered a bed of fire to be made, and walked across it to prove her word. At this point in the re-enactment her followers do likewise.

PHOENIX

All these receive their birth from other things
But from itself alone the Phoenix springs.
Self-born, begotten by the parent flame
In which it burns, another yet the same.

Its allotted span of life now fulfilled
Its nest on oaken boughs does it build,
Or trembling tops of the sacred palm,
Of cassia, cinnamon and stems of nard.

And there does rest till ethereal flame
First catches, then consumes the priceless frame;
Consumes it too as on the pyre it lies.
It lived on perfume and in perfume dies.

An infant Phoenix from the dead one springs,
Its parent's heir with outspread wings,
Greets the dawn with song and bathes in dew
And a fresh lease of life on the same terms renews

Immunity to fire is widely seen as a mark of virtue and even saintliness, and one of the holiest creatures of all is the legendary bird that dies and is reborn in flame.

The legend of the Phoenix tells us that when the Deluge drowned the world one part only was saved. Far in the East where the mountains touch the sky, the waters rose and rose until at last they held still, leaving just the tallest peak as an island above the lapping waves for that was the only place untainted by the evil of the world. And in that island was a garden where spring reigned eternally, where the sun never set and all creatures were at peace with one another. In that garden was no hunger or thirst that could not immediately be quenched, no sorrow or pain, no death to rob joy of its sweetness. Here as in Eden the lion lay down with the lamb and the eagle nested with the dove, and all creation grew to a beauty beyond our imagining.

The source of all this joy was the Fountain of Eternal Youth that stood in the midst of the garden, from whose crystal waters all the creatures drank and all the trees and flowers and trailing vines were watered. Known also as the Well at the World's End, it was this wonder that Alexander sought in his great adventure, and failed to find despite conquering the world. For when the waters of the Deluge fell and life began anew in the world, the way to the garden was sealed to mortal eyes. Had Alexander been planted at the very gates of the garden he would have seen only emptiness.

One creature alone in this paradise was mortal, and it was the only one of its kind in all Creation - the Phoenix, supreme among birds. Somewhat like an eagle in appearance, the Phoenix was the most beautiful and revered of all feathered kind. Crimson and gold was the plumage of its head, breast and shoulders, while its wings and tail shimmered with all the colours of the rainbow. When the Phoenix opened its beak to sing, all the other creatures hushed to listen, for its song too was the most beautiful in creation. And although it resembled the eagle, the Phoenix was no hunter because it fed

◁ **Phoenix**
Roger 1993
Oils 15 x 23in (38 x 58cm)

purely on air and incense, and was at peace with all other beings.

The Phoenix was the most beloved and blessed of the birds of Paradise, but alone among them it was still doomed to die. Every five hundred years (or some say a thousand or even more) the bird feels age and weakness stealing through its veins. Then it knows the time has come for returning to its place of birth. Taking leave of the others in the garden, the Phoenix soars down from the mountains at the dawn edge of the world and follows the sun westwards, riding the high winds across India and Persia and Arabia. And all the birds of the world flock around and trail after the Phoenix in its flight, hunter and hunted alike, so that the people of the world gaze up in astonishment and know again that the legends are true.

In the heart of Arabia the Phoenix settles at last in the boughs of a great palm tree, some say the Tree of Life itself. There it builds a nest from cinnamon, spikenard, myrrh and all the other fragrant incenses of the Arabian desert. Then it lays down with the setting sun and lets Time take possession of its being. By dawn it lies completely still and there is no flicker of life in its eyes. Then the sun in his passage across the sky gazes close with his fiery eye upon the Phoenix. Fumes and vapours begin to rise from the cinnamon so that the air around the palm tree grows sweet with perfume. Then at noon the vapours ignite and clear flames spread crackling through the woven nest. It becomes a funeral pyre on which the dead Phoenix blackens and is consumed.

Some say the fumes of incense close round the dead Phoenix in a shell, so after a time it seems that an egg sits there amid the flaming nest. Then as the flames subside there comes a crack as the shell splits and there rises with glorious song a new young Phoenix that breathes greedily of the perfumed air, and grows fiercely with each breath.

In three days the bird is fully grown. Then it gathers up the nest and the ashes of its old self in its claws and flies south to the Temple of the Sun in Egypt, accompanied by all birds that have heard rumour of its coming. At Heliopolis, the Phoenix lays down its burden on the roof of the temple or a nearby crag before turning east, mounting up through the sky on fresh wings till even the eagle is left far behind. So the Phoenix comes back at last to Paradise, which its eye alone can see and which it alone of mortal creatures can enter.

For much of history the Phoenix was believed to be real. In 34 AD the Roman historian Tacitus, not noted for his flights of fancy, recorded that the Phoenix had at last been seen again in Egypt: 'attended in its flight by a group of various birds, all attracted by the novelty and gazing in wonder at so beautiful an apparition.'

With variations in detail the Phoenix was anciently known in legend through wide tracts of the Americas, Europe, Africa and Asia. In China it was one of the Four Most Fortunate Creatures who assisted at the creation of the world, along with the Unicorn, Dragon and Tortoise. Known as the Feng Huang or Red Bird of the South, the Phoenix shared many characteristics with the Unicorn. Both were benevolent and the friend of all other creatures. The sighting of either was taken as a blessing on the rule of the current emperor and was entered carefully in the official chronicles.

Where the Dragon represented the Emperor in the Chinese court, the Phoenix represented the Empress. If you are lucky enough to spot a Phoenix in China, they say you will find treasure nearby, because the bird takes pleasure in lifting people's burdens.

6

ELEMENT WATER

APHRODITE

WATER SPIRITS

BRIGID

RUSALKI

In astrology Water, along with Earth, is considered a passive element as opposed to the active principles of air and fire. It is considered emotional and intuitive, and through its association with the zodiac sign Cancer is closely linked to the moon. This fits what we have seen elsewhere. The moon and ocean are plainly linked by the tides and certainly in Europe most wells, springs, streams rivers and lakes have a patron goddess or nymph.

APHRODITE

When Cronos agreed to overthrow his father Uranus, Gaia armed him with a sharp sickle and, as Uranus lay sleeping, Cronos crept in and severed his genitals, which were thrown into the sea. The blood from the terrible wound sank into the earth and gave birth to the fearsome Furies, to giants and the Meliae, the nymphs of sombre ash-trees. By contrast, the severed parts turned to white foam on the ocean wave, amid which was born in time the beautiful goddess of love, Aphrodite. Zephyrus, the benevolent West Wind blew her ashore on the Isle of Cyprus, where she has been held in special reverence ever since and where she was greeted by the Horae (the Seasons). They clothed her in jewels and sumptuous robes and led her to the assembly of immortals on Olympus, where all the male gods immediately wanted to marry her.

Seeing this, Hera and several other goddesses were jealous of her sweet, winning beauty. This came to a head at a feast attended by all the immortals save Eris, whose name means Discord. Furious at not being invited, she tossed into the assembly a golden apple with the inscription: 'For the Fairest'. Hera, Athene and Aphrodite each reached for it and an argument immediately followed.

◁ **Night Bathing**
Linda 1994
Pastel 6 x 6in (15 x 15cm)

To settle the dispute Zeus decreed that they submit the question to an impartial mortal. So Hermes (Mercury) led the three goddesses to Paris, son of King Priam of Troy. Paris was tending his father's flocks on Mt Ida in Phrygia and was not at all happy at being chosen to judge the matter. However, he had no choice. Each of the goddesses appeared in turn and each tried to sway him by offering a reward. Hera promised him power, Athene offered victory in battle. But Aphrodite offered him the hand of the most beautiful of mortal women, and it was to her that Paris awarded the golden apple. This was how he came to win the love of Helen of Troy. But he also won the enmity of the other two goddesses, who saw to it that Paris lost the famous war which followed his elopement with Helen.

However, once they had satisfied themselves with revenge on Paris, the other goddesses gradually became reconciled to the new beauty in their midst, and accepted that in this respect at least Aphrodite outshone all others, both divine and mortal.

Known to Romans as Venus and to the Babylonians as Ishtar, Aphrodite became one of the most popular of the Greek goddesses. She is credited with having countless affairs with both gods and mortals. Officially she was married to Hephaistos, the crippled master craftsman of Olympus, but she rarely let this restrict her amorous adventures. On one occasion Hephaistos built an ingenious cage and trapped his wife in *flagrante delecto* with Ares (Mars), the god of war. Then he demanded justice from Zeus for her adultery, but the

◁ **Venus** (detail)
Linda 1991
Oils 11 x 21in (28 x 51cm)

other gods just laughed at him. But before one feels too sorry for Hephaistos, he had a famously roving eye (and other organs) himself, so he probably got no more than he deserved.

All the immortals loved Aphrodite when they did not happen to be furious with her. The trouble was, she was always far more interested in getting involved, and getting others involved, in amorous adventures than in their outcome, which was often tragic. Hera was her particular enemy on Olympus because of all Zeus' romantic straying, for which Hera held Aphrodite responsible almost more than Zeus himself. But even Hera generally forgave her in the end because although often mischievous, causing grief was rarely Aphrodite's intention, which was simply to lighten people's hearts with the delicious joys of love.

As goddess of love, Aphrodite was worshipped under three guises: Aphrodite Urania (the Celestial), goddess of pure or ideal love such as that which inspired knights in the Age of Chivalry; Aphrodite Genetrix, the patroness of married couples; and Aphrodite Pandemos or Porne, the goddess of lovers, mistresses and courtesans.

WATER SPIRITS

Aphrodite rose from foam on the ocean wave but the oceans were already well populated in the Greek imagination by a multitude of deities and other spirits. Chief of them all was Poseidon (Neptune), god of the underwater world who had displaced Nereus, the original 'Old Man of the Sea', who thereafter became a purely benevolent deity who helped sailors in distress. Nereus dwelt in a palace in the depths of the Aegean Sea where with his wife Doris he fathered the fifty Nereids, the original mermaids. Their male counterparts were the Tritons, sons of Poseidon and Amphitrite, supreme goddess of the ocean.

The Nereids gave way or evolved in time into the mermaids of popular legend who until quite modern times were believed perfectly real. For many an age sailors fully expected to encounter mermaids out at sea and there are countless tales of mermaids being seen on rocks near the coast, combing their long tresses, admiring their own reflections in mirrors and singing with such eerie beauty that men immediately fall in love with them. There are many tales of marriages between men and mermaids, with or without their fishtails. To this day in the Scharrzfeld Jurisdiction in Germany there is said to be a fund for the poor called the Brauhard Account, set up by a Lauterberg man called Brauhard in memory of his mermaid wife, who lived in a bathtub in his house till she was poisoned by intolerant neighbours.

Celtic folklore is as full as any of mermaid tales but in Scotland and Ireland it is believed mermaids can take on fully human form when they shed the seal-skins they wear to swim from their underwater realm to ours. Any man who finds such a skin and hides it away can claim the mermaid for a wife when she comes looking for it, and there are many tales of lonely bachelors finding a wife this way. The mermaids or Merrows are said to make very good wives and mothers, but if they find the hidden skin, which they invariably seem to in the end, they will use it to abandon their family and escape back to their own realm.

◁ **Waiting for the Tide**
Linda 1997
Oils 7 x 9in (18 x 23cm)

BRIGID

In the Scottish Highlands and Islands the rebirth of nature is celebrated on Candlemas, or St Bride's Day on 1 February. The tradition has weakened but the same feast has been celebrated since time immemorial. At its height, bonfires were lit on hilltops and there would be a festival with some young maid crowned with candles and honoured in Brigid's stead. Candles were lit in every windows and homes in the Isles were decorated with early flowers and greenery. Bride's Crosses or Wheels were woven from corn and hung around the house.

Women would also make a crib with a mattress of corn and hay. They called it Bride's Bed and into it they tucked under a blanket a straw doll representing Bride, and beside her a wooden club. The crib was laid near the door surrounded by glowing candles. Food and drink were laid on the table and a decorated chair set by the hearth. Then just before they went to bed, the women of the house would call out three times: 'Bride is come, Bride is welcome!' Or they would go to the door and cry out into the night for Bride to enter their house.

Next morning everyone would search the ashes of the hearth, hoping to find an impression of Bride's club. If they did it was the sign that they would have prosperity and a good crop in the coming year. The weather that day was also watched closely because, as the old saying has it:

If Candlemas day be fair and bright, Winter will have another flight.
If Candlemas day be shower and rain, Winter is gone and will not come again.

St Bride's day, wherever it is celebrated, is one of the clearest examples of a pagan festival being adopted by Christianity because even the name has not changed. St Bride or Brigid simply took over the mantle of the pagan Brigid, chief goddess of not only the ancient Irish but Celts across a wide swathe of western Europe. The name in Gaelic means 'bright flame'. In northern Britain she was called Brigantia, chief deity of the Brigantes tribe who were often led by warrior queens. Elsewhere she was called Brigit, Bride, Brighid, Brigandu and Berecynthia.

Whatever the precise spelling, Brigid was a triple goddess. Or, as it was sometimes put, there were three sisters all called Brigid who were the patronesses respectively of fertility, poetry and smithcraft.

As goddess of fertility Brigid was concerned equally with humans, animals and vegetation. Everywhere she walked, flowers sprang up under her feet. In her shrine it was always springtime and her herds never ran dry of milk. Brigid was the patroness of midwifery and of healing generally. She was particularly associated with sacred springs and holy wells, to which people would bring prayers and offerings to ward off disease and barrenness. These wells were adopted by her Christian successor and many continue to be places of pilgrimage today.

As goddess of poetry, Brigid was keeper and dispenser of inspiration, the 'fire of the soul'. The symbolism of water and fire is combined in the Cauldron of Inspiration, of which she is the keeper. She invented the Ogham alphabet and it is said of both pagan and Christian Brigids that they were struck in their

forehead on birth by a shaft of fire from heaven.

As goddess of earthly fire, the third Brigid was the patroness of metalcraft and all smith-work. In legendary battle her preferred weapons were the spear and arrow, and indeed one interpretation of her name is 'Flaming Arrow'.

Brigid's festival was one of the four main events in the ancient Celtic calendar because it marks the invisible rewakening of Nature within the cold earth. It was also sometimes called 'Oimelc, Ewe's Milk' because it opened the season of lambing.

On Brigid's Night the maiden goddess of fruitfulness and abundance replaces the sombre hag (Cailleach) who took possession of the year at Samain (Hallowe'en or All Saints Night). The grim goddess of reckoning and mortality is replaced by the smiling one of hope, full of virginal gaiety, beauty and promise.

In Christian Ireland St Brigid is said to have been baptized by St Patrick himself. Later she founded the Abbey of Kildare where she worked many wonders. Along with Patrick and St Columba she became one of the three patron saints of Ireland. Sometimes called Mary of the Gael, she was made patron saint of poets, blacksmiths and healers.

St Brigid seems to have been a real person but her legend and name blend so neatly with her pagan predecessor's that one suspects some embellishing of the truth. Or perhaps she was, as her early followers must have believed, a fresh incarnation of the goddess, born into the Christian era to continue her ministrations within the new order. This is hinted at in the tales of St Brigid being weaned on milk from a white, red-eared cow. These were the colours of the Tuatha's creatures.

She was born in Uinmeras, about five miles from Kildare, on 1 February 453AD, or so it is said. Her father was Dubtacht (or Duffy), a pagan noble who may also have been a druid. Her mother was Brocessa, his Christian slave.

Within a fenced enclosure at St Brigid's Abbey of Kildare (or Cill Dara, the Church of the Oak), which no man was permitted to enter, there was kept alive a sacred fire. From St Brigid onward it was tended by nineteen nuns, each being responsible for a day at a time. On the eve of the twentieth day the last nun would place logs by the fire with the prayer: 'Brigid, guard your fire, this is your night.' And so she would.

This ritual survived from ancient times when nineteen vestal virgins, or kelle, had tended the flame. They were virgins, though, in a much looser sense than their successors. On occasion they would take male pilgrims into their beds and conceive children by them. These children were given the surname 'Kelly' and supported by Brigid's community. It's doubtful that the Christian nuns continued this practice, but curiously many churches dedicated to St Brigid supported families named Kelly or O'Kelly until modern times, paying all their baptismal fees.

St Brigid was notable among abbesses of the time for having the power to appoint her local bishop. And he was always a goldsmith. Many remarkable miracles of healing took St Brigid's Abbey. One story tells how two lepers came to the sacred well at Kildare hoping to be cured. Brigid told one of them to wash the other, which he did and the disease peeled away from his skin. Then she told the cured one to likewise bathe his friend. But he shrank from

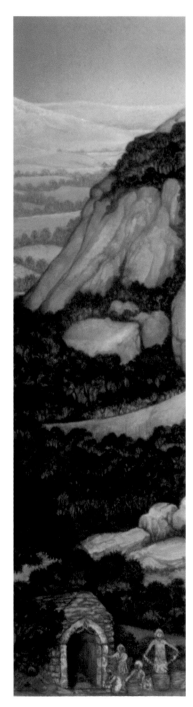

touching the diseased flesh. So Brigid herself bathed the man and cured him. Among the wonders of Kildare that Gerald of Wales recounted was the creation of an illuminated manuscript said to have been dictated to the scribe by an angel in response to Brigid's prayers. Of the decorations Gerald famously wrote: 'If you take the trouble to look very closely, and penetrate with your eyes to the secrets of the artistry, you will notice such intricacies, so delicate and subtle, so close together and well-knitted, so involved and bound together, and so fresh still in their colourings that you will not hesitate to declare that all these things must have been the result of the work, not of men, but angels.'

In 1220, some forty years after Gerald's visit, a Norman-appointed Bishop grew angry at the exclusion of men from the Abbey at Kildare. Arguing that nuns were subordinate to priests, he demanded the gates be opened to allow inspection. When the nuns refused, the Bishop's men forced their way in, declared the sacred flame to be a pagan superstition (quite correctly of course) and extinguished it. It was later rekindled and kept alive till Henry VIII's Reformation when it was once again put out, more or less finally. Despite being one of the three patron saints of Ireland, St Brigid's authority has been steadily eroded through the ages by the Catholic Church, culminating in her de-canonization in the 1960s. Along with St George of England, the Vatican decided there was insufficient proof of her sanctity. Or, indeed, of her existence.

At Kildare today Brigit's ancient fire temple is marked by the Cathedral of St Brigid. Along with many of the most grand churches in Eire still, it is an Anglican establishment, a legacy of colonialism towards which the Catholics seem remarkably tolerant, given that only three per cent of the Republic's population is Anglican.

The Cathedral itself is a pleasing building of pale grey stone, more four-square than most churches and with a tall round tower in one corner of the precinct. Beside the cathedral a rectangular enclosure marks the ancient hearth, with a sign saying 'St Brigid's Fire Temple' (some anomaly here perhaps?). But there are few other concessions to the place's ancient pre-eminence. The cathedral might still be dedicated to St Brigid but it celebrates her in a very muted way.

Within the church there are large stained glass portraits in the main aisle of Patrick and Columba but St Brigid is banished to a small window high in the central tower. This is pleasing enough in itself and shows Brigid with the famous flame on her brow, but you get the impression of St Brigid having been politely but firmly put in what the Church thought of as her place i.e. distinctly subordinate to her male counterparts. In the west window she appears again, apparently, but not very obviously. The rest of the windows have an overwhelmingly masculine tone. Similarly it is only the altar in the north transept that is obviously dedicated to her, with a Brigid's Cross hanging on the tapestry above it. The cross is possibly echoed in the tile pattern of the main floor but that's it, really.

However, if one is not feeling too militant on Brigid's behalf it is, a very pleasant cathedral and it is something that the 'Fire Temple' has not simply been ploughed over. For a taste of true Brigid fervour one has to go to Bride's Well a mile or so downhill in the rough direction that her statue in the marketplace is

gazing (next to a bull-fertility testing station, ironically, or perhaps fittingly). Here an oak sapling can be found dressed with holy medals and scraps of cloth. Nearby grow the reeds from which true Brigid's Crosses are woven.

The Christian legend goes that St Brigid first wove one of these while keeping vigil by her father's sickbed. When Dubtacht asked the meaning of it she explained the Gospel to him, whereupon, according to the tale, he saw the errors of his ways and became a Christian.

RUSALKI

Oh come, lonely hunter in the stillness of dusk,
Come, come! I miss you, I miss you!
Now I will embrace you, embrace you!
Come, come! My nest is near, my nest is near.
Come, come, lonely hunter, now in the stillness of dusk.

This is the song of the Rusalki, who in Russia and neighbouring countries are said to be water nymphs who hibernate in nests in their underwater palaces during the winter and emerge from lakes and rivers and streams soon after the Spring Equinox. Then they can be seen combing their long hair on the banks and disporting in the water, tempting any young man who passes by to join them. After a few weeks they move from the water into the weeping willows and other trees nearby and beg scraps of linen from passers-by, which they carefully wash and spread in the sun to dry. Later they will use them to line their underwater nests along with the flowers, straw and feathers which they collect for the same purpose. These are the offerings people make to them when trying to coax their goodwill.

In southern Russia the Rusalki are considered to be benign fertility spirits, though young men have to beware of joining their games because they are likely to become so besotted they will want to go and live underwater with the nymphs and not see their families again. It is said that from seven weeks after Easter the Rusalki go wandering through the ploughed fields singing and clapping their hands, usually invisible save for the waving of the corn in their wake. By moonlight they also dance visibly in the fields and this encourages the crops to grow.

As nature spirits, the Rusalki have influence over the winds and rain, so farmers carefully cultivate their favour with offerings of garlands of flowers and ribbons thrown into the water. Maidens make the same offerings in the hope of obtaining rich and handsome husbands. In appearance the Rusalki are very beautiful with pale skin, slender bodies, soft musical voices and long wavy hair. Their eyes are dazzling and they are usually naked or clad only in wreathes of mist. They enjoy riddles and often any young man wishing to enjoy their favours must first unravel their cunning puzzles.

The souls of stillborn babies and those who die unbaptized are said in southern Russia to be taken by the Rusalki to live happily in their underwater palaces as compensation for not entering the Christian heaven.

△ **Brigid**
Linda 1992
Oils 12 x 14in (30 x 35cm)

In northern Russia they hold much the same beliefs about Rusalki but viewed from a very different slant. There they say the Rusalki are totally malevolent, that they lure young men into the water only to drag them down to a watery grave, and they dance in the fields only to ruin crops or steal the grain. Any man who gets caught up in the dance will never recover. Even if he survives he will have gone mad.

The northern Rusalki's eyes are blank and have an uncanny green glow. They may still be beautiful but it is the sickly, cadaverous beauty of the siren or vampire. Offerings are made to them with the purpose of deflecting their evil attention elsewhere rather than coaxing their blessing. Woe betide those with no gift for the Rusalki when they meet them, or who carelessly muddy the scraps of cloth they have spread out to dry. If it is a farmer, his crops will fail and all other fertility drain from his life. If it is a young man they will lie in wait for him and lure or simply drag him underwater. If it is a young woman she will be cursed with barrenness and die an old maid.

In the north they say Rusalki are the spirits of drowned maidens, particularly suicides and those who have died by violence. When the body of such an unfortunate is found, an attempt is made to prevent her becoming a Rusalka by staging a grand funeral with plentiful offerings of food, wine and vodka being laid beside the body.

The northern Rusalki are also said to enjoy riddles, but the penalty for failing to solve them is being tickled to death or otherwise tortured before being drowned. Swimmers are warned to wear a crucifix around their neck or carry a sprig or leaf of absinth because these ward off the Rusalki; but at night sometimes even these charms fail.

Rusalki are said to be married to the Vodaniye who are bloated, horrendously ugly monsters that have no apparent saving graces at all. The Vodaniye feed on those who drown and store their souls in jars in their crystal palaces. Drowned maidens can avoid this fate only by marrying them and thus becoming Rusalki, whose duty it is to secure fresh

victims. Vodaniye also lurk by the water's edge themselves ever hunting for fresh souls. Most often they haunt millponds and all over Russia at one time pigs or even horses were fattened up and thrown into millponds weighted with stones to appease the Vodaniye's appetite and prevent them attacking the mills, which they hate. Sometimes even passing strangers were pushed in.

In southern Russia Rusalki are also sometimes believed to be married to Vodaniye, but they hate them and this is why they look out for handsome young men to disport with. In all regions the Rusalki are believed to retreat to their palaces with the first snow and are not seen again till spring. They can take the form of owls to avoid recognition.

◁◁ **Rusalki (south)**
Linda 1997
Oils 4.5 x 12in (11 x 30.5cm)

◁ **Rusalki (north)**
Linda 1997
Oils 4.5 x 12in (11 x 30.5cm)

7

BIRTH & DEATH

Birth and death are the greatest events in most lives, the milestones and ultimately the bookends of our personal drama. In the presence of both we touch the infinite, the irrevocable. By its very nature birth is the province of the Goddess since the female principle is the gateway by which new life enters the world. There is a particular fascination, then, with goddesses who seek to destroy life, because this appears to betray that principle.

SIRENS

Sirens are the ultimate *femmes fatales*. People generally imagine them as lethal mermaids using their charms and irresistible song to lure passing sailors onto the rocks, but the original sirens of Greek myth were very different in appearance. The earliest illustrations on Greek pottery show them as birds with human heads, of whom the goddess Circe warns Odysseus:

'Your next encounter will be with the Sirens, who bewitch everybody that approaches them. There is no home-coming for the man who draws near them unawares and hears the Sirens' voices; no welcome from his wife, no little children brightening at their father's return. For with the music of their song the Sirens cast their spell upon him, as they sit there in a meadow piled high with the mouldering skeletons of men, whose withered skin still hangs upon their bones. Drive your ship past the spot, and to prevent any of your crew from hearing, soften some beeswax and plug their ears with it. But if you wish to listen yourself, make them bind you hand and foot on board and stand you up by the step of the mast, with the rope's ends lashed to the mast itself. This will allow you to hear with enjoyment the Sirens' voices.'

◁ **Sirens**
Linda 1997
Oils 4 x 5.5in (10 x 14cm)

Odysseus does this and duly goes mad with desire when he hears the singing but, as instructed, his men only tighten his bonds each time he begs to be set free, so they safely pass by the danger. The island was said to be in the Ionian Sea and the number of Sirens varies in different accounts from three to nine. There are conflicting accounts of their origin but their shape is said to have come about when, as Persephone's companions when she was stolen by Hades, they asked Zeus for wings so they could search for her.

Originally the Sirens were not malevolent at all. They were seen as kindly guides of souls to the land of the dead and their images often appear on ancient tombs and coffins accompanied by a lyre or double flute. Possibly they were embittered or cursed as a result of losing a singing contest with the nine Muses, much as Medusa was cursed by losing a beauty contest with Athene. Their wings resembled those of owls, a bird form adopted by female vampires around the world.

There is a parallel between the Sirens in the Odyssey and the Birds of Rhiannon, whose songs are so enchanting that years can pass by without their listeners noticing. The difference is that Rhiannon's birds do not eat their audience. Rhiannon is a mostly benevolent Welsh goddess, but like Danann in Ireland she has a very distinct dark side.

RHIANNON

Rhiannon enters the Mabinogion in the tale of Pwyll, Prince of Dyfed. Near Narberth, where Pwyll had his court, was a hill called the Mound of Arberth of which it was said that anyone who sat upon it would have a strange adventure. One quiet day, Pwyll decided to test this for himself. With his followers he went and sat on the Mound and soon saw a beautiful female dressed in cloth of gold ride by on a pure white horse. Pwyll was struck with wonder and sent some courtiers after her; but no matter how fast they rode, she always kept just ahead without ever seeming to quicken her pace. By this they guessed that she came from Annwn, the supernatural realm.

Pwyll was undaunted because he had once spent a whole year in Annwn and had good friends there. The following day he ascended the Mound again, and again she came riding by. Pwyll chased her himself but no matter how furiously he rode, she always effortlessly kept just ahead. Finally he called out and begged her to stop.

'Gladly,' she replied, reining in her mare. 'And it were better for your steed if you had asked sooner.'

She introduced herself as Rhiannon, daughter of Hevydd Hen (which means the 'Ancient Man'). She explained that against the will of her family she had fallen in love with Pwyll and would marry no-one else, even if Pwyll rejected her. Well, Pwyll could hardly hope to hear better because by now he had fallen in love with her himself, so they agreed that a year from that day Pwyll would go to Annwn to claim her hand. This he did and after various adventures finally succeeded in taking her home to Narberth to rule happily beside him.

All went well and in time Rhiannon grew heavy with child. Then disaster struck. On the night she gave birth to a boy child, she and her six attendants fell asleep. When the servants woke they found the baby missing. In panic they

killed and dismembered a staghound cub, smeared Rhiannon with blood and scattered the remains over her bed. When she woke they told her she had devoured her own child in a fit of madness.

Despite everyone's horror, Pwyll's love was such that he would not put her away, but as penance Rhiannon was made to stand at the horse-block outside Narberth, tell her dreadful tale to each arriving stranger and carry them into the castle on her back as though she were a mare.

Luckily in Gwent Is Coed there lived a lord called Teirnyon who had a related problem. He possessed the most beautiful mare in the world but every year when she foaled on May Eve, the foal vanished without trace. At last Teirynon decided to sit up with the mare and see what happened. When the colt was born a long, clawed arm came in through a window and laid hold of it. Teirnyon hacked the arm off at the elbow with his sword. There came a dreadful howl which Teirnyon pursued out into the night without luck, but when he returned he found a baby boy there wrapped in silk swaddling.

Teirnyon and his wife raised it as their own. Then they heard the tale of Rhiannon's woes, and looking closely at the child they saw how much he resembled Pwyll Prince of Dyfed. So they returned him to his parents and amid great rejoicing he was named Pryderi, which means Trouble. And Pryderi in time became Prince of Dyfed himself and the hero of many tales.

In this tale we meet Rhiannon in her positive aspect, the victim of injustice which is doubly so because she is a goddess who has chosen to marry a mortal. The fact she does not question the possibility that she devoured her own baby hints at the darker side of her personality. In this negative aspect Rhiannon is the fatal white mare whose nest is lined with the bones of dead poets. She is the night-mare who consumes those who drink from the 'cup of divine inspiration', but lack the wisdom , strength and virtue to bring the visions into fruition. The 'cup of divine inspiration' was a literal thing, a cauldron or goblet in which herbs were brewed to produce a trance-inducing mix, allowing seers to penetrate the veil between the worlds. Then as now the failures probably vastly outnumbered the successes.

◁ **Nightmares** (detail)
Linda 1976
Oils 9 x 9in (23 x 23cm)

Vivien

A storm was coming, but the winds were still
And in the wild woods of Broceliande
Before an oak, so hollow, huge and old...
At Merlin's feet the wily Vivien lay.

As a horse-goddess Rhiannon was worshipped throughout Celtica as Epona, the white mare who wears a crescent moon as her necklace and has nine daughters almost identical to herself. In her human guise Rhiannon has been equated with the Arthurian Lady of the Lake, Nimue or Vivien, who seduced Merlin in his dotage in order to steal his secrets.

Vivien or Nimue is an ambivalent figure in the myth of Arthur. As one of the Ladies of the Lake (possibly even *the* 'Lady of the Lake') she is Arthur's otherworldly patroness, much as the Morrigan attached herself to the hero Cuchulain in Ireland. Nimue provided Arthur's sword Excalibur and saved him on several occasions from Morgan le Fay's treacherous plots. From time to time she guided him with advice and warnings and was one of the females who sailed his body to Avalon after the final battle, in which he was slain by evil Mordred. Yet she is perhaps best known for her beguiling and betrayal of Arthur's wizard Merlin for the sake of his ancient wisdom, for Merlin was not just a wizard in his own right but was an incarnation of the patron god of Britain, the Isle of the Mighty.

Merlin, having the gift of prophecy, knew very well that his infatuation with the maiden Nimue would lead to disaster, but like many another old man he could not resist the spring-like grace of her youthful beauty. He knew it would end in tears but was powerless to resist the charm of her immediate presence. According to Malory he told King Arthur that he was doomed to pay for his passion by being buried alive. Arthur protested that surely with all his craft and wisdom Merlin could avert this, but Merlin simply shook his head sadly. He went wandering with Nimue widely and little by little she wormed the secrets out of him. Often Merlin was tempted to use enchantments to have his wicked way with her (because the worst of it was that while she tempted and teased him mercilessly, she would not actually sleep with him), but in a weak moment Merlin had promised never to do this and felt bound by his oath.

Accounts vary of how it all ended. Some say that when she had learned enough, Nimue finally wheedled out of Merlin a certain spell of enchantment which she used to imprison him in a hawthorn bush, which for the Celts were fairy trees often inhabited by those who can pass between the worlds; or an invisible tower of air or glass. Malory says that in a final bid to win her heart, Merlin promised to show her a great wonder hidden underground in a cave. She persuaded him to lead the way, then sealed the entrance with rocks and spells which not even Merlin could undo. And there in his crystal-lined cave at Clas Myrddyn he remains to this day, caught between life and death.

This is the most common account, though arguments have raged over the location of Clas Myrddyn, ranging from the Scottish Lowlands to Bardsey Island off north Wales, a hill near Carmarthen in the south (which was Merlin's original home, and where it was long believed that when Merlin's Oak in the centre died, so too would the town) and even across the Channel in Brittany in the magical Forest of Broceliande.

△ **Merlin** (detail)
Linda 1996
Oils 11 x 16in (28 x 41cm)

◁ **Summoning a Lover**
Linda 1996
Oils 15 x 17in (38 x 41cm)

Xochiquetzal

In Mexico and other Central and South American regions we first think of the malevolent aspects of their deities - all those human sacrifices so vividly depicted in surviving manuscripts and the tales of the Conquistadors; but that is to forget the part human sacrifice plays at some point in most cultures. Caesar enjoyed castigating the Gauls for their practice of ritual human sacrifice, but in Rome itself it had been common till not long before. In a way it even continued long afterwards in their public games in the forums, even though the new god was simply that of popular unrest.

Which is not to condone human sacrifice of course, just to apply a little perspective. The religions of Central and South America were regrettably addicted to human sacrifice from our point of view, but people are much the same everywhere. Apart from the unfortunate victims themselves, we can surmise that the myths and religions in Pre-Columbian America served much the same ends as in the rest of the world, and life for most people contained much the same blend of love and hate, light and darkness.

The Aztec goddess of love was known by different names in different places but was commonly called Xochiquetzal. She dwelt in a beautiful garden in the ninth heaven, also called the Paradise of the West, with the god of flowers and crops. He is often shown as a jaguar embracing the Tree of the West, a form of the goddess herself. This tree is sometimes depicted with red and white stripes spiralling up it and fruit sprouting from the tips of the branches, as in the fig tree. Xochiquetzal's consort was said to be the planet Venus, though originally she was married to the sun. The maize plant was said to have come from this western paradise as a gift from the divine couple.

Surviving descriptions of Xochiquetzal bear a strange likeness to those of the Japanese Amaterasu. Like Amaterasu she has a rich palace and many attendants who spend much time spinning and embroidering wonderful garments. Her own quarters are called the House of Birth which is full of flowers and cool breezes. Every year she was honoured throughout the lands of her dominion with a great festival. Flowers from the goddess' garden have the property of inspiring love many times greater than any earthly flower, so when they fell to earth all kinds of adventures followed. As with Venus, Xochiquetzal was as much the patroness of illicit and casual love as of that sanctioned by marriage, so her festival was often a rather wild carnival.

As a love goddess Xochiquetzal was not naturally in favour of hermits and ascetics. So when one of them seemed in danger of storming the heights of heaven, the other deities would send her to teach them a lesson. One tale that has survived is that of a man called Yappan who, like an Asian Hindu decided to abandon his family and go into the desert to meditate on a holy rock till he achieved enlightenment and immortality. The gods sent many temptations his way but he resisted them all, to the point where they felt they might be forced to grant his ambition. Then the goddess of love went to him in person. Looking up at the gaunt ascetic, she praised his grit and determination and said she had come to comfort him after his ordeal. But first, could he help her climb up to his place? So Yappan came down to lend a hand and what with one thing and another he soon fell hopelessly under her spell. For his presumption he was turned into a scorpion and has been hiding in shame ever since.

Fertility Goddesses

The Mother Goddess is the source of all life. Other powers can preserve, shape or destroy it but without the female principle there is no life to organize, merely barren emptiness. In ancient times recognition of this went far beyond gratitude for individual human existence. Observing nature it was plain that the same thing happened on all levels. It was the female that brought forth new life and generally nurtured it until it could fend for itself. Even the plants were male and female. To our ancestors it must have followed that even inanimate things were created in a similar way.

And who can dispute this? Mechanistic explanations for the creation of matter carry a certain dreary conviction that in a sense they are right, but they often sound like someone trying to analyse a musical symphony by dismantling the radio which happens to be playing it, hoping to find the answer somewhere in among the transistors and microchips. One is left with the question: 'So what happened just before the Big Bang that prompted the explosion?'

The suggestion that life began with an egg floating in the formless void seems as valid as any. Which suggests that since eggs are the exclusive property of females there was in the beginning a primal goddess within whom it took shape. People were no less intelligent in ancient times, they just had less information at their disposal and a different mental landscape. What is surprising is that physicists today, with all their vast store of knowledge have so far come up with no better suggestion for the origin of the universe than ancient philosophers.

Details vary, as we have seen, but most spontaneous mythologies begin with a Mother Goddess out of whom, for hazy reasons, was born the world of opposites, male and female, light and dark, sky and earth, good and evil. Immediately after their separation the opposites are then set spinning by the principles of love and sensuality. Aphrodite and her attendant Eros, mischievous though they often are, also represent the magnetic attraction between opposites that causes them to reproduce in the myriad forms that creation has taken. Often defying all logic and sense, love as personified in Aphrodite is the essence that keeps the opposites from simply flying apart.

Then when new life is born comes the nurturing aspect of the Goddess, the caring, milk-providing, hearth-warming pillar of stability. The ancient Egyptians pictured one aspect of the Great Mother or Nut as Hathor, the great cow whose milk provided nourishment for all things. The moon itself was a pool of her milk and scattered across the sky it formed the Milky Way. In other cultures it was said that the earth was formed on the primal waters by churning the great Goddess' milk till it solidified like butter. Pots and cauldrons were sacred to the Goddess partly as symbols of her creative womb, partly as containers of the divine milk that sustained all things. The Asian Artemis of Ephesus had four hundred breasts to feed her varied children impartially and irrespective of the conflicts between them.

△ **Muse of Love**
Linda & Roger 1995
Oils 18 x 18in (46 x 46cm)

◁ **Cypress**
Linda 1988
Oils 4 x 10.5in (10 x 27cm)

BANSHEE

In Ireland they have a particular goddess who attends the death of important people. In the old days this meant kings and queens, but with the passing of native Irish monarchs the Banshee continued to perform her services for any similarly important personages provided they were Irish, or had the best interests of Ireland and her people at heart. The name Banshee or Bean Sidhe means 'woman of the hill' because it is in the fairy mounds of Erin that she lives, along with the rest of the fairy people. Her main dwelling is at New Grange on the River Boyne, burial place of the High Kings and Queens of Ireland and site of the main palace of the Tuatha de Danann when they ruled the country. Whether there is just the one Banshee or several is uncertain, but probably like other Celtic goddesses she is quite able to multiply herself at need.

The Banshee warns of the impending death of any in her care with a legendary screech heard by the family and others close to the person. Often she appears visibly too, either around their dwelling or to travellers on their way there. As with all fairy activity, appearances of the Banshee have declined drastically since the start of the twentieth century, but what is remarkable is how active she was until then. Even more remarkable is that in latter days she would screech, keen and show herself at the death of Catholic priests and Protestant clergymen if they had served their congregations well, given that she is a pagan goddess of whom neither branch of Christianity has ever really approved.

The Banshee is generally a dreaded being, but only because humans are naturally terrified of death itself. She is in fact one of the guardian spirits of Ireland and she marks the passing of great people out of respect for their deeds in serving their country, irrespective of their creed.

In the eighteenth century an eyewitness of the Banshee described her appearance as: 'a tall, thin woman with uncovered head, and long hair that floated round her shoulders, attired in something which seemed either a loose white cloak or a sheet thrown hastily about her.' The same witness, a Miss Barry of Castle Barry in County Cork, who related the incident in a letter to her sister in October 1752, said of the Banshee's shriek: 'If it resembled anything earthly, it seemed the cry of a female struck by a sudden and mortal blow, and giving out her life in one long, deep pang of expiring agony.'

We all fear death. Few of us can face it with equanimity and a sense of our life's cup having been so satisfyingly drained to the full that we are eager to move on to the next stage. But while such witnesses as Miss Barry inevitably perceive the Banshee from this side of that fear, the chances are that the person actually dying sees her very differently, because the name Banshee means 'beautiful lady of the Sidhe' and some philologists have even traced a common root to the name Venus (Ban becomes Bhan which becomes Van in Gaelic pronunciation). It is even reported by some witnesses that the Banshee has appeared in the form of a beautiful young woman rather than a spectral and unnerving wraith, and that her song is beautiful.

Besides politically important people, the Banshee attends the death of great artists because music, poetry and the visual arts are if anything more important to the fairy people than politics, and they feel a special kindred to those with talents in that direction. In the old days anyone with such talents was believed to owe them to the people of the Sidhe.

◁ **Ghost Stories** (detail)
Linda 1997
Oils 12 x 8in (31 x 20cm)

8
GOOD & EVIL

CIRCE

PANDORA

MEDUSA

THE MORRIGAN

Among the opposites released into the world at Creation were good and evil, which were shared equally between goddesses and gods. Exactly what the dynamic is between them, and why evil should be a necessary part of things are not questions we intend to try and unravel here. As no-one else has ever got satisfactorily to the bottom of them it would be presumptuous to try, but it does no harm to poke our noses a little way in..

Many of the darker aspects of the Goddess seem genuine enough. For every specifically feminine virtue there is bound to be a corresponding vice and for every bright goddess there is bound to be a shadowy being embodying the exact opposite. But many have a ring of propaganda or projection about them. Witches are a famous case in point. In the heyday of witches there must have been evil ones among them, just as there are evil people in all walks of life, but their furious persecution in the sixteenth and seventeenth century just proves how subtle evil can be, and how easily it disguises itself as righteousness and virtue.

The goddess Circe, whom we consider next, is a bit of a puzzle to know which side of the fence she is on. She starts as a demonic scourge of passing sailors then suddenly switches to being all sweetness and light with no real explanation being offered for it. As Homer's Odyssey is almost our only source of information on her we are left to guess the reason. Had she been slighted in love by some god or mortal? Did she have some wager going with the god Hermes? Decide for yourselves.

◁ **Witches**
Linda 1987
Oils Ø 16 in (40.5 cm)

CIRCE

△ **Circe**
Linda 1986
Oils 10 x 10in (26 x 26cm)

In his famous eighteen year sea voyage home from the Trojan War, Odysseus visited Aeaea, the island home of beautiful Circe, daughter of Helios and Oceanid Perse. Having just escaped near total disaster with only one surviving ship, Odysseus and his men lie recovering on the beach for two days, having no idea where they are. On the third morning Odysseus sets off to reconnoitre the place and returns dragging a dead stag behind him. They roast it gratefully and when they have eaten their fill Odysseus tells the others what he has found. 'My friends', he says, 'when I climbed a crag to reconnoitre, I found that this is an island and for the most part low-lying, as all around it in a ring I saw the sea stretching away to the horizon. What I did catch sight of,

right in the middle, through dense oak-scrub and forest, was a wisp of smoke.'

After recent harrowing encounters with the Cyclops and the like, no-one is very keen to investigate. But they need supplies so in the end lots are drawn and a party of twenty two set off. In time they come to a well built stone palace guarded by mountain wolves and lions. Seemingly guarded, that is, because instead of attacking the mariners the beasts run up and fawn on them like hounds greeting their masters. Terrified anyway, the men back into the palace gateway and hear a beautiful female voice singing within. This is of course Circe weaving at her loom one of the shimmering, delicate fabrics that goddesses love to make.

They shout for help and in a while the polished doors open and there stands the most beautiful female they have ever seen. She invites them in and they gratefully enter, all save Eurylochus who is leader of the party and is suspicious. The goddess leads the rest into her hall, settles them on couches and offers them a dish made of cheese, barley-meal and golden honey flavoured with Pramnian wine. Not having eaten since their breakfast, the sailors are ready for such a delicacy and tuck in with relish, oblivious that Circe has also sprinkled into the dish a magic potion of her own devising. Soon they feel intoxicated and forget who they are and where they come from, and even their own names. Circe waves her wand and turns them into grunting pigs condemned to wallow in sties.

Eurylochus sees enough of this to guess what has happened and races back to tell the others. Odysseus slings his bow over his shoulder, sets his great bronze sword in its silver scabbard and sets off for the palace alone. His remaining men beg him not to, saying they can only hope to save their own skins, but he will not be dissuaded. In the woods near the palace a youthful stranger falls in with him, whom Odysseus recognizes as the god Hermes, or a messenger in his likeness. 'Where are you off to now, my poor fellow' says Hermes, 'wandering through this strange land with your friends penned like pigs in Circe's sties? I suppose you intend to try and free them, bold hero that you are. Lucky for you that I am here to help you or you would surely end up like the rest.'

Hermes plucks from the ground a herb called Moly, with a black root and a milk-white flower and gives it to Odysseus, explaining that it is an antidote to the potion Circe mixes for her guests. He explains that Odysseus should eat the potion, then when Circe raises her wand he should draw his sword and threaten to kill her. He explains a few more things too that must be done if he is to release his friends from the spell. Odysseus follows the instructions to the letter. He knocks at the palace door and follows Circe in. He settles down on a beautiful chair decorated with silver and rests his feet on a stool placed there for him. He drinks her pottage from the golden bowl she gives him. Then when she taps him with her wand and orders him off to the sties with his friends, he draws his sword and threatens to kill her.

Circe falls to her knees: 'Who are you?' she cries. 'What parents and what city begot such a man? For never before has any man drunk of my potion without falling into my power. You must indeed be Odysseus, that Hermes warned me would one day come in a black ship. But I beg you now, put up your sword and come to my bed, so that in love and sleep we may learn to trust one another.' Odysseus answered, 'How can you expect me to trust you when just now you would have turned me into a pig like my friends. And how should I come to your bed when in the helplessness of love and sleep you might still betray me?' So then Circe swore by her honour as a goddess that she would do him no harm, just as Hermes had said. Then Odysseus allowed himself to be bathed by the nymphs who attended Circe and went willingly enough to her soft bed.

Later Circe freed Odysseus' friends from their enchantment, and when he fetched the rest of the company from the shore they found the former pigs enjoying a banquet in the hall, bathed, anointed and wearing fine robes. When the two companies came face to face and each man recognized his friends, they burst into tears and fell into each other's arms, till finally the goddess beseeched Odysseus to calm them: 'I know as well as you' she said, 'all you have suffered on your voyage from monsters and savages and the ill-favour of the gods. But now I want to see you enjoying your food and wine till you are once more the men you were when you first sailed from your homes in Ithaca. You have all forgotten what it is to have a merry heart, so now put aside your cares and be my guests until you remember.'

They needed little more encouragement and settled down to a feast that lasted a whole year, by which time they felt restored and eager to be getting on with their voyage home. So one day they went to Odysseus and begged him to remember their true purpose and do something about getting them home. For the rest of that day till sunset they sat and banqueted on the meat and mellow wine that were provided in such abundance. When the sun sank and night fell, Odysseus' men settled down for sleep in the darkened hall. But he went to the beautiful bed where Circe lay and there clasped the goddess' knees in prayer.

'Circe' he said, 'I beg you to keep the promise you once made to send me home. I am eager now to be gone and my men wear me out with complaints when you are not there.' 'Royal son of Laertes, Odysseus of the nimble wits, I am not going to keep you in my house against your will. But before I can send you home you have a journey of a very different kind to make. You must find your way to the Halls of Hades and Persephone the Dread, to consult the soul of Teiresias, the blind Theban prophet.'

This is not at all what Odysseus wanted to hear, but he is past suspecting the goddess of any treachery and follows her commands, becoming one of the very few humans to visit the underworld alive and return to tell the tale. In Hades Odysseus learns many useful things from a broad perspective. Then he and his men return to Aeaea and Circe gives more immediate advice about the dangers they face in getting home. Among them the perils of the Sirens and Scylla and Charybdis. Without Circe's advice they must surely have all perished, so in the end when they take leave of her, Odysseus and his men have every reason for gratitude.

What is not made clear by Homer in the Odyssey is the cause of Circe's general hostility to men at the beginning, because it is plain by her change of attitude that she is not particularly evil. Also not explained what happens to all the other wild beasts that are enchanted men.

Pandora

According to one Greek tradition, man and all the animals were created by the Titans, Prometheus (he who has foresight) and Epimetheus (he who has hindsight). Prometheus modelled man from clay and his own tears, but when it came to bestowing special talents on him, so he could rule all creation, he and Epimetheus found they had already given out all such talents to the animals. So Prometheus stole fire from the forge of heaven (or possibly the sun) as a gift to man that gave him mastery over the earth. Prometheus paid dearly for this theft because Zeus eventually sentenced him to be chained to Mt Caucasus where an eagle tore at his liver all day, and it renewed itself at night only so the torture could continue. Eventually Zeus relented and allowed the hero Hercules to set the Titan free.

Pandora was created from clay in heaven by Hephaistos the master craftsman as a companion for the Titans. The four winds breathed life into her and all the goddesses and gods contributed to her fashioning. Aphrodite gave her beauty, Hermes gave her eloquence, Athene gave her dexterity and so on. She was called Pandora, the All Gifted, and one of her particular gifts was curiosity. Pandora was sent to Epimetheus who was delighted to have so lovely and talented a companion.

Now in Epimetheus' workshop was a jar or box in which he stored all the things he did not want in creation, or thought unnecessary. He warned Pandora not to open it, but neglected to tell her why. The question of what might be in there began to prey on Pandora's mind till finally she just had to take a peep. But soon as she opened the lid there rushed out like a noxious gale a host of plagues and diseases, and Spites such as hatred and envy, malice and greed that had not been known in the world before. Pandora snapped back the lid, but too late. All that remained in the box was Hope, which had not been needed before because creation was perfect.

Thus did evil and suffering come into the world through curiosity. This was the start of the mythical Bronze Age of war and famine. After a while Zeus got so fed up with the world that he raised a great flood to destroy it. Only two beings survived. They were flame-haired Pyrrha, Pandora's daughter by Epimetheus, and Deucalion, Prometheus' son. Prometheus warned them of the coming flood so they built an ark. For nine days and nights they floated on the raging waters till coming to rest at last on the twin peaks of Mt Parnassus. Through them the world was populated again and Pyrrha found Pandora's Box, from which she released Hope.

There is another version of the story in which Pandora brought the box or vase with her to earth and it contained a bridal gift from each of the deities on Olympus. She opened it too soon and they all escaped except Hope, which has remained our comfort ever since. In many ways this makes more sense, but the most famous part of Pandora's tale is the release of all evil into the world.

Still a third version says that Pandora was created by Zeus as a deliberate revenge on the Titan brothers, that she was sent to earth with her box or vase filled with evil (and a strict injunction not to open it) because Zeus knew that sooner or later curiosity would get the better of her. This most hostile version of the myth is the best known, but it appears to have been largely invented by Hesiod as a deliberate anti-feminine parable.

Medusa

Medusa was once a beautiful maiden whose chief pride was her glorious flowing hair. She was so beautiful that she dared stand against the goddess Athene in a beauty contest. For this presumption the goddess blighted her looks and turned her tresses into a writhing nest of hissing snakes. Her once sparkling eyes grew stony and dull. So hideous and embittered did Medusa become that any person or animal who looked upon her was turned to stone. The whole region around the cavern where she dwelt was littered with what seemed statues of those who suffered this misfortune, and people abandoned the country for fear of her.

Medusa was sister to the Graea, three hags who had been grey-haired from birth. The Graea had only one tooth and one eye between them, which they passed around and each used in turn. When the hero Perseus decided to try his strength and luck against the Gorgon Medusa, he first visited the sisters to get directions from them. They refused but Perseus snatched their eye as it was being passed from one to another, and would not return it till they gave what he asked.

So concerned were the gods that Perseus should succeed in this challenge that they had equipped him themselves. Athene, his special patron, had lent him her invulnerable shield made from the skin of the marvellous goat Amalthea. Hermes had lent his winged sandals and a charmed sickle with which to strike the blow. Hades had given a magic helmet that rendered the wearer invisible (though some say Perseus stole this from the Graea) and a magic wallet.

Thus armed, Perseus flew to the westernmost extremity of the earth where Medusa dwelt and crept into her lair while she was sleeping. Not daring to look directly at her, but guiding himself by reflections in the bright boss of his shield, Perseus crept up and cut off her head with a single mighty blow. Some say that Athene guided his hand to make sure of it. From the monstrous wound sprang the wonderful winged horse Pegasus, who was later to become the bearer of Zeus' thunderbolt and Aurora, the Dawn.

Putting the head in Hades' wallet, Perseus mounted on Pegasus' back and flew off till at sunset he happened to find himself in the land of rich Atlas, tallest and mightiest of the Titans in whose garden grew the legendary golden apple trees. Perseus landed at the palace and asked for hospitality, claiming this by right of being a son of Zeus and the hero who had just conquered Medusa. Atlas, remembering a prophecy that a son of Zeus would one day come and steal his golden apples, turned him roughly away. A struggle followed which Perseus appeared to be losing until, averting his own gaze, Perseus whipped out the Gorgon's head and held it up to the Titan. Atlas was turned to stone, but he did not become a statue like other victims. Instead he grew till he became what are still called the Atlas Mountains in Africa that carry the weight of heaven on their shoulders.

In a similar fashion Medusa's head was to prove useful in other adventures, one of which provided Perseus with his wife Andromeda; but when he returned the deities' gifts Perseus presented it to Athene. She mounted it on her shield so anyone who faced her in battle afterwards was turned to stone.

▷ **Medusa**
Linda 1998
Oils 18.5 x 24in (46 x 61cm)

◁ **Morrigan**
Roger 1998
Oils on paper 14 x 20in (36 x 51cm)

The Morrigan

The Morrigan was the main battle goddess of the ancient Irish. The name means either 'Great Queen' or 'Queen of the Phantoms'. She is one of the more frightening Celtic goddesses, though in an age when warfare was the main instrument of political change, she was far from being seen as simply evil. She was an instrument of fate and conductor of souls to the afterlife, so she was often the warrior's friend. As a triple goddess she was more or less a mirror image of Danann or Brigit. While Danann was mostly a benevolent, kindly deity, she did have an aspect known popularly as Black Annis, which was terrifying. The Morrigan by contrast was mostly fearsome and delighted in the fury of battle, but her activities often resulted in unexpected blessings and regeneration.

As a triple goddess the Morrigan's three avatars are Badb (crow), Nemain (Frenzy), and Macha (which also means crow or raven). Collectively these three are called the Morrigan. They influence the outcome of battles through magic or enchantment rather than direct means. A favourite ploy is to trick friends and allies into fighting each other. Or else they paralyse the will at crucial moments, something every warrior dreads. The Morrigan often adopts the guise of hooded crow or raven, the frequenter of battlefields, but can also appear as a very beautiful woman or, more commonly, a hag or Cailleach. As a member of the Tuatha De Danann, the Morrigan helped them to victory against both the Fir Bolg and the Fomorii in the two Battles of Moytura (Mag Tured). After the Tuatha retreated into their fairy mounds the Morrigan would be called upon by all warriors about to enter battle.

The Morrigan is the dispenser of both courage and fear, which often decide the outcome of battle more than physical prowess or weaponry. In this she is related to the Valkyrie of Teutonic myth. She is also of course the goddess of victory and all its sweet joys, including the fertility that follows bloodshed.

The legendary Irish warrior Cuchulain, the 'hound of Ulster', perished in the end because he failed to recognize and acknowledge the Morrigan. When he was single-handedly defending Ulster against Queen Maeve and an army drawn from the rest of Ireland, a young woman in a coat of many colours came and declared her love for him. She was, she said, a king's daughter and her love had been woken by the tales of his heroism. Cuchulain roughly told her he had no time for thoughts of love just then.

'It will go hard with you then,' she told him. 'For when you are fighting your enemies' champion in the ford, I will be the eel that trips you up and drags you under.' Then she vanished and when he saw a crow on a branch nearby Cuchulain knew he had just spoken with the Morrigan.

His impatience and her enmity were to cost him dear because, as she had warned, she was his enemy from then on. She finally had her revenge when in the guise of three old hags she tricked him into breaking his personal taboo or gessa against eating dog flesh. This was the main instrument of his downfall and the cause of his losing courage at the crucial moment. When Cuchulain lay dead the Morrigan settled on his shoulder in the form of a crow. The moral that has often been read into this and similar tales is that if men will not master or come to terms with war, it will master them. Anyone aspiring to be king had to have the goddess of war on his side. If Cuchulain had recognized her, or simply accepted her offer of love, he may well have become king of Ireland. or

◁ **The Battle**
Roger 1998
Pen and ink (actual size)

9

LESSER DEITIES

True Thomas lay o'er yon grassy bank,
And he beheld a lady gay,
A lady that was brisk and bold,
Come riding o'er the ferny brae.

Her skirt was of the grass-green silk,
Her mantel of the velvet fine,
On every lock of her horse's mane
Hung fifty silver bells and nine.

True Thomas he took off his hat,
And bowed him low down on his knee:
All hail thou mighty Queen of Heaven!
For your peer on earth I ne'er did see.'

O no, O no, True Thomas,' she says,
That name does not belong to me;
I am but the queen of fair Elfland,
And I'm come here for to visit thee.'

◁ **Fay**
Linda 1996
Oils and collage 21 x 28in (53 x 71cm)

The fairy people have always played a lively part in the imaginations of the people of the British Isles. As we have seen, in Ireland the god-like Tuatha of pagan times evolved into the Sidhe who inhabited fairy mounds and a hidden realm to which these mounds and certain other places like St Patrick's Purgatory were gateways. They were long believed to be very real, occupying an order of being halfway between humans and angels, with whom they were easily confused.

As we also briefly saw earlier there were believed to be other fairy realms beneath the waves, populated by a variety of supernatural beings besides mermaids, who were often not seen as fairies at all but creatures as solid and fleshly as humans.

SELKIES

In Scotland the mermaid is called Ceasg or Maighdean no Tuinne 'maiden of the wave'. She is said to resemble a human female to the waist and a salmon below. If caught, she may be persuaded to grant three wishes. She seems able to shed her tail because there are fables of marriages between Ceasg and humans, and their sons became great navigators. Like other mermaids, some are dangerous sirens who lure men under the waves to drown.

In the Orkney and Shetland Islands people tell of Selkies or seal maidens. These are semi-magical creatures of human form who live in underwater palaces. To swim from their world to ours they don seal-like skins, which they hide when they come ashore. If a man finds the skin of a Selkie maiden and hides it elsewhere, he may claim her for his bride. Often she will live with him for years and bear his children, but in the end he usually breaks some taboo, or she finds the skin and goes home. Selkie males, conversely, come ashore to seduce human maids, whom they will generally leave at the first chance. The offspring of these unions have webbed fingers and toes. When the blood of a Selkie or mermaid is shed in the sea, storm rises. Selkies and merpeople are separate but there is friendship between them. From the Shetlands comes a tale of a young seal hunter who was out at sea with several companions. Skinning one of their catch, he is horrified to find it is a Selkie. He keeps the skin but quickly thows the body overboard. Unknown to him, the Selkie is still alive, though freezing without her fur. Sinking into the depths, she happens to drift into a mermaid's cave. The mermaid decides to help her by getting the skin back. Bravely she allows herself to be caught in the seal-hunter's net and hauled aboard. The young man is horrified again and begs his friends to throw her back, but they refuse and want to sell her ashore. They lay her on the Selkie fur and head for port, but the mermaid's skin dries out and she dies. A storm blows up and the ship is wrecked. The Selkie's skin drifts down to the cave where she is hiding, and in it she manages to swim home as a seal once more.

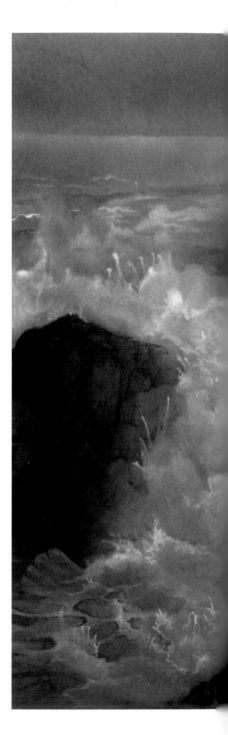

▽ **Selkie** (detail)
Linda 1989
Oils 14 x 9in (36 x 23cm)

Sphinx

There is a legend in Egypt about the famous Sphinx near the pyramids of Giza. It is said that before Thothmes IV became Pharaoh he was out hunting one day in the desert. Exhausted after chasing a gazelle in vain through the blazing heat, he took shelter at noon in the shadow of the sphinx, which was then already two thousand years old and was buried up to its neck in sand. Maybe it was the sun or maybe he fell asleep, either way Thothmes suddenly looked up in alarm and the head, with a halo of the noon sun, came alive and spoke to him: 'I am Ra, god of the sun,' it said. 'I am Khepera and Atum and many other names unknown to men. I am the guardian of this land of Egypt, bestower of the double crown upon Pharaohs.'

Then in the vision Ra, through the mouth of the statue, promised Thothmes that he could be Pharaoh if he promised to restore the worship of Ra, which had declined, and among other things to restore the statue of the sphinx to its former honour and glory. All of which came about. Thothmes became Pharaoh and one of his first accomplishments was to clear the sand of centuries from around the great statue and build a temple for the worship of Ra between its paws.

There are statues of various kinds of sphinx found throughout the Middle East and eastern Mediterranean, with a lion's body, human head and sometimes wings. In Egypt the heads are male, but the ancient Greeks pictured the sphinx as having a female head and breasts and she was almost always winged. In Egypt the sphinx was a guardian of the dead as well as being an embodiment of Ra and a symbol (for reasons that are now obscure) of the annual inundation of Egypt by the Nile. It was basically a benign creature, however awesome. In Greece and Rome she was seen as hostile and wantonly destructive. There was a famous sphinx said to haunt the main road leading to the city of Thebes. Her habit was to lie in wait on Mt Phocium for travellers and ask them a riddle she had learned from the Muses: 'What creature walks on four feet in the morning, on two feet at noon and on three feet in the evening?'

Then when they failed to give the right answer she would tear them apart and throw them over the precipice on which she was in the habit of sitting. As a result of this the road was soon little used, until one day along came Oedipus, he of the famous complex. Oedipus, although he did not know it, was the rightful

heir to the throne of Thebes, so when the sphinx pounced and asked her riddle, the Muses inspired him with the answer. 'Man is the creature,' Oedipus replied. 'For man creeps on hands and knees as a child, walks on two legs as an adult and with the aid of a staff in his dotage.'

The sphinx was so furious she threw herself over the edge and was smashed on the rocks below.

The Muses

The Muses who came to Oedipus' aid were most commonly said to be the daughters of Zeus and the Titaness Mnemosyne, which means Memory. After the triumph of the Olympian deities over the Titans, his sisters and brothers asked Zeus to create some deities to celebrate the victory fittingly. So Zeus visited Mnemosyne and slept with her for nine consecutive nights. In due course she gave birth to nine daughters who formed the Choir of the Muses. With their wonderful singing they often entertained the company at feasts on Mt Olympus, but they dwelt on forested Mt Helicon in Boeotia. There they were guardians of the many springs and pools, including the sacred fountain Hippocrene which was opened by a kick from Pegasus' hoof. Beside these pools they danced tirelessly, singing all the while. In the evenings they left the mountain and wandered abroad in a cloud of mist, when their wonderful singing was often heard by humans.

On Olympus the charm of their song often soothed the great gods and goddesses, turning anger to smiles and jealousy to forgiveness. But they were not above a little jealousy of their own when their primacy was threatened. As we have seen, they cursed the Sirens (daughters of the Muse Melpomene) for daring to challenge them, and when the bard Thamyris challenged them to a poetry contest they first of all defeated him, then struck him blind and dumb. The nine daughters of the Macedonian king Pierus were changed into magpies for daring to challenge the Muses to a poetry contest.

Mostly, however, the Muses were sweet and charming and gentle and the effect of their singing was to spread peace and harmony among humans and gods alike. To begin with they were virgins but later they had many love affairs and their children also did much to further the cause of music in the world. Calliope gave birth to the famous musician Orpheus, and Terpsichore produced Linus who was believed to have invented melody and rhythm.

Although they generally performed as a group, each of the Muses had a specific area of interest. Calliope, who has given her name to carnival organs, was their leader and the Muse of epic poetry and eloquence. Clio was the Muse of history, Erato of romantic verse, Euterpe of flute-playing, Melpomene of tragic drama, Polyhymnia of heroic verse and mimicry, Terpsichore of choral song and dance, Thalia of comedy, and finally Urania was the Muse of astronomy and navigation.

The Muses often accompanied Apollo in his role as god of music. Near his palace on Mt Parnassus was the spring Castalia which was sacred to them and whose waters were said to inspire poetry and even prophecy in those who drank them. The Castalia waters were drunk by the Pythian oracle at Delphi before she prophesied, and used in other purification rites there.

◁ **Sphinx** (detail)
Linda 1979
Oils 17 x 24in (43 x 61cm)

When Hermes invented the lyre from a tortoise-shell, he fitted it with nine strings in honour of the Muses and made a gift of it to Apollo, who gave him the caduceus, the messenger's wand with two snakes entwined round it, in exchange.

ELVES AND TROLLS

In Scandinavia they have very similar traditions about the fairy folk as in Scotland. They are generally called huldre folk or elves, a term which spread to Scotland and England but was apparently no more popular with those to whom it was applied than the term 'fairy' itself. They preferred to be called 'good neighbour' or 'wight', according to this traditional Scottish rhyme anyway:

> *If you call me imp or elf,*
> *I warn you to look well to yourself;*
> *And if you call me fairy,*
> *I'll work you much great worry.*
> *But if 'good neighbour' you call me,*
> *Then good neighbour I shall be;*
> *And if you call me 'Seelie wight',*
> *I'll be your friend both day and night.*

In Scandinavia they are divided into light elves and dark elves, equivalent to the Scottish Seelie and Unseelie Courts who were forever at war. They are generally smaller than humans, though this is only noticeable when large numbers are gathered. The light elves have kings and queens and love singing and dancing. They shun daylight so their twilight dances in the woods go unseen, leaving their 'fairy rings' in the grass. If a man stumbles upon them dancing in the moonlight he will be so entranced by the beauty of the elf maidens that he will be rooted to the spot. And this is good because if he joins the dance he will lose either his life or his sanity because the frenzy of the dance is too much for mortals to bear.

Huldre girls are very beautiful and wear grey dresses with white veils but often it seems they suffer the strange affliction of having tails like those of cows, which is the only way it can be told that they are not human. In one story a man dancing with an elf maid notices the tail peeping out from her hem, but instead of giving her away he just tactfully tells her that her garter is slipping. In gratitude she ensured that he was rich for the rest of his life.

Another strange defect afflicting some Scandinavian elf maidens is that while they appear very beautiful from the front, from the back they look like hollow and rotten trees. Dark elves like these are mischievous and in the old days were fond of stealing food, drink and even babies, who were replaced with changelings. This was once every new mother's great fear and elaborate rituals were performed to prevent it happening.

Light elves are purely benevolent by inclination. There are countless tales of them returning favours many times over and often it seems they ask favours of people simply to test them and see if they are worthy of fairy favour. They are only to be feared if they are insulted or injured in some way. Humans who unwittingly damage their fairy homes or otherwise offend them will be warned and given fair chance to mend their ways before retribution begins. Dark elves however like nothing better than to torment humans, and because of the difficulty of distinguishing them from the others, and the danger of getting caught up in their wars, Scandinavians have generally tended to steer clear of the elvish folk as far as possible.

Besides the huldre folk, Scandinavian mountains and forests are also inhabited by trolls of various types. Those of the forests, the men and women 'of the woods' tend to resemble the trees they live amongst. Their bodies are hairy as if covered in moss and their skin as gnarled as the bark of pine trees. Often hunters and woodsmen almost pass them by, taking them for the stump of some dead tree. They are apparently not unfriendly if approached in a respectful manner. They speak the human tongue, though slowly, and if they take a liking to a human will reveal the secrets of herbs. Many famous herbal remedies are attributed to them.

Trolls of the mountains are best avoided however. They are sullen and foul-tempered, fond of conjuring storms and casting boulders down on travellers. They are close relations of the giants of Jotunheim who lusted after Freya and made war on Thor and the other gods of Asgard.

◁ **Hags** (detail)
Linda 1976
Oils 9 x 9in (23 x 23cm)

Dryads

Dryads are wood nymphs who live in trees, but they can leave them in the form of beautiful young maidens who were often courted by the gods in ancient Greece, particularly Apollo who had a special affection for them. They also often accompanied Artemis in her hunting. In Italy and Greece it was common until recently for maidens to knock on the trunks of certain trees and ask the spirit within to reveal to them the name of the youth they would marry, and they would sometimes hear it whispered in the rustling of the leaves, or hear an answering knock from within that they could interpret.

Certain trees were said to be inhabited by nymphs called hamadryads who could not leave them. Hamadryads were human only down to the waist where they merged inextricably with the trunk and roots. They were chained to their tree and when it died, so did they. Such hamadryad trees usually only grew in secluded and remote places where men rarely came upon them. If one did, and tried to cut the tree down, a shriek was heard as the axe bit through the bark. The nymph Daphne became a hamadryad when, fleeing from Apollo's unwelcome passion, she begged her father, the river god Peneus, to save her virginity and he did so by turning her into a laurel tree. Grief-stricken, Apollo adopted the laurel as his totem and instituted the custom of crowning victors in the Olympic Games with laurel leaves.

There was once a grove of trees sacred to the goddess Demeter wherein grew a mighty oak that was a hamadryad tree which towered above the rest and spread its branches so wide that from a distance it looked like a small forest in itself. Around it the dryads of the other trees danced and sang in honour of the great oak and Demeter, and people from afar brought offerings to thank the goddess for their harvests.

All this honour annoyed a certain lord called Erisicthon who decided to cut the tree down. One day he arrived with his servants armed with axes and wagons to cart the wood away. The dryads, seeing what he intended, all flocked around begging and pleading with the men to spare the oak. The servants hesitated but Erisicthon seized an axe from one of them and swung it with a mighty blow that cut deep into the wood. A groan came out of the tree and blood flowed from the wound. One of Erisicthon's men pleaded with him to stop, and paid for it with his life. Erisicthon faced the tree and raised the axe again. A voice came out of the tree saying: 'Erisicthon, my life is dear to Demeter. I warn you that if you slay me, you will pay for it dearly.' But the lord was determined and rained blows upon the tree till with a mighty wail it crashed to the ground, bringing down much of the grove with it.

The nymphs fled to Demeter and told her what had happened. Demeter bowed her head in grief and all the corn in the fields bowed with her. Then Demeter sent a messenger to Famine in the distant wastes of Scythia; and Famine went to Erisicthon in the night and embraced him and breathed her essence into him so that when he woke his stomach was filled with a raging hunger such as can hardly be imagined. Erisicthon fell to eating as though he were an army. He ate until all his wealth was consumed in trying to feed him. He sold his own daughter to buy food and finally, when he had nothing left to sell and nothing else to eat, he began eating himself and did not stop till death finally released him from the curse.

◁ **Cypress** (detail)
Roger 1998
Oils 15 x 36in (38 x 91cm)

▷ **Echidna and the Sphinx**
Roger 1991
Oils 20 x 15in (51 x 38cm)

CONCLUSION

The main conclusion that springs to mind at the end of this book is that it is a shame it is not twice as long. Exhausted though the three of us are at this particular moment, it also feels that we have barely dipped our heads below the surface of the subject. There is so much more to investigate, illustrate and say. Beyond Nut there is Isis whom we barely had space to more than mention. Greek and Celtic goddesses have had a fair showing but we have hardly touched upon the Hindu ones or those of Africa and America. Patterns have emerged but even more have beckoned from the margins, such as the mystery of trees.

However, in other ways it has all pulled together better than we could reasonably have hoped at the outset; and there were times when distractions made it questionable that we would ever see this day when it is finally all complete and ready to be packed off to the printers. The joy about Goddesses as a theme is that they have been so much neglected and overshadowed, so there is a certain freshness in bringing them to the forefront and viewing myths from their perspective. It throws a new light on familiar tales and has led to many odd and delightful discoveries that it has been a pleasure to unearth and share.

Most of the pictures in this book are new. Linda especially has many other goddesses paintings which could easily have been included but she chose instead to take this chance to explore fresh themes. The overall plan of the book is largely hers. Roger and I made our contributions, but for the most part we were happy to let her set the pace and general direction. My own particular hobby-horses at the beginning were Lilith and Brigid, but beyond them and what general curiosity suggested along the way, I was happy just to follow the course laid down by the basic divisions of the book. Amaterasu was a particular treat and arose simply because we were looking for sun goddesses and she was the most lively of those we found.

Personal thanks go to my immediate family, Viv and Lorna, for their patience, especially over the last few weeks of the project when I might just as well have been living on the moon. Also to Linda and Roger for the pleasure of working with them again, and at the end of it having something to pick up and feel proud of.

◁ **Veiled Voices**
Linda 1988
Oils 6 x 6in (15 x 15cm)

Acknowledgments

Briggs, Katharine, A Dictionary of Fairies (Allen Lane, 1976)

Bulfinch, Thomas, The Golden Age of Myth Legend (Wordsworth Editions, 1993)

Davidson, H. R. Ellis, Myths and Symbols in Pagan Europe (Syracuse University Press, 1988)

Frazer, James G., The Golden Bough (Macmillan, 1929)

Graves, Robert, The Greek Myths (Pelican, 1966)

Graves, Robert, The White Goddess (Faber Faber, 1990)

Gregory, Lady, Irish Myths and Legends (Running Press, 1998)

Harding, M. Esther, Woman's Mysteries (Rider Co, 1977)

New Larousse Encyclopedia of Mythology (Hamlyn Books, 1987)

Rees, Alwyn and Brinley, Celtic Heritage (Thames Hudson, 1994)

Rolleston, T.W, Myths and Legends of the Celtic Race (Constable, 1987)

Ross, Anne, Pagan Celtic Britain (Constable, 1992)

Quotes

Page 53   Greek Hymn, 'Hail, gentle dawn!..'

Vedic Hymn, 'Ushas is the first of all to wake..'

Page 56   Flaccus, 'Like fiery clouds..'

Page 62   Homeric Hymn, 'Hestia, in the high dwellings of all..'

Page 68   Ovid, 'All these receive their birth..'

Page 87   Alfred, Lord Tennyson, 'A storm was coming..'

Page 107   Traditional Scottish Ballad, Thomas Rymer.

Paintings

Page 38   'Winter', Brian Curry.

Page 39   'Spring', Nick Roberts.

Page 40   'Summer', Brian Curry.

Page 41   'Autumn', Mrs.R.Robinson

Page 46   'Frost', Mr. and Mrs. Scawn.

Page 64   'Firewalkers', Brian Curry.

Page 70   'Night Bathing', John Knights.

Page 91   'Muse of Love', Mr. and Mrs. Scawn.

Page 102   'Selkie', Brian Curry.

Thanks to the people listed above who purchased or commissioned these original paintings used in She, the Book of the Goddess.

▷ **Goddesses**
Linda 1998
Oils 7 x 7in (18 x 18cm)